The Story of
BRISTOL

BRYAN LITTLE

Edited and revised by John Sansom

HALSGROVE

First published in 1991,
revised edition published by Redcliffe Press in 1999,
new edition published by Halsgrove in 2003

BRITISH LIBRARY CATALOGUING IN PUBLICATION DATA
A catalogue record for this book is available from The British Library

ISBN 1 84114 301 4

HALSGROVE
Halsgrove House,
Lower Moor Way,
Tiverton, Devon EX16 6SS
Tel: 01884 243242
Fax: 01884 243325
www.halsgrove.com

Printed by Bookcraft Ltd., Midsomer Norton

Contents

Acknowledgements

The publishers are grateful for permission to use
illustrations appearing on the following pages.

Bristol City Museum and Art Gallery:
34, 37, 38, 44, 46, 52, 53, 55, 56, 57, 78

Bristol Record Office: I

Bristol Tourist Information and
Marketing Centre: II, III, IV, V, VI, VII, VIII

British Aerospace: 84, 87

Bromhead Photography: 52

John Laing and Son Ltd: 89

National Monuments Record: 8

National Portrait Gallery: 18

John Trelawny-Ross: 18, 85

Medieval Beginnings

Bristol, originally Brig-stow, comes from an ancient word which means 'the place of a bridge'. At some time in the long Anglo-Saxon period some enterprising people – perhaps the inhabitants of an existing small town on the Avon – decided to make it easier for travellers to cross the swirling and disagreeably muddy river which parted them from the other, still undeveloped side. That first bridge was almost certainly of timber, a material in which the Anglo-Saxons were expert workers, and was probably thrown across the Avon in the tenth century. By this time most of England was a unified kingdom; the earlier Anglo-Saxon kingdoms such as East Anglia, Wessex and Mercia having been absorbed into one.

Bristol stood on what had been the Mercian side of the river. Early in the eleventh century it became part of Gloucestershire; it also occupied the south-western tip of the large area, including a hunting ground of the Saxon kings, in what later was known as the Forest of Kingswood. For church purposes it was in the Midland diocese of Worcester, founded about AD 680 and throughout the medieval period including Gloucestershire as well as Worcestershire. On the other side of the bridge the low-lying area, ending in the sandstone ridge known as Redcliffe, was in Somerset and in the diocese of Wells. This division of Bristol between two counties lasted till 1373, and the ecclesiastical division persisted till the reign of Henry VIII.

The small town of Bristol was contained between the Avon and its much smaller tributary the Frome (a common name for rivers in the West of England), which flowed down from the countryside of southern Gloucestershire. The Avon became important to the small ships of those days as a river port, with traffic to other ports along the Bristol Channel and also to southern Ireland. The town could have served this shipborne traffic, and probably acted as a shopping and resting place for the travellers, on foot or using pack-horses, who crossed the bridge on their journeys between Gloucestershire and Somerset. The inhabitants would have traded with those travellers and offered them refreshment. Churches – perhaps only St Peter's (whose parish stretched into the countryside to the east) and St Mary's by the Harbour (later known as St Mary-le-Port) – would have served their worshipping needs.

Because traders needed a supply of ready money a mint was set up in Bristol, as in other trading towns, under the control of the kings of what was now a unified England. The inscription on a coin of about AD 1000 (now in Stockholm) stamped with the name of the official in charge, Aelfwerd, says that this 'moneyer' was 'On Bric'.

The last years of the Anglo-Saxon period were probably uneventful in Bristol, and the town seems to have submitted, peacefully enough, to William the Conqueror in the autumn of 1066. But two years later, when there was still campaigning elsewhere in the West of England, including a siege of Exeter, the bastard sons of Harold, who had taken refuge with the Norse colonists in Dublin and Waterford, tried to stage a 'come-back' and attacked Bristol. But they were repulsed by the townsfolk, who were probably content with the stability and good order now established by the first of the Norman kings.

A year before William the Conqueror's death the Domesday survey gives details of 'Barton in Bristow'. The area which one could describe as 'Barton' has the details one would expect from an agricultural area running out, over the countryside east of the town, as far as Stapleton and Mangotsfield. The bordars, or smallholders, are mentioned; so too are the villagers, the free tenants, and those with servile status. Ploughs are mentioned, also two mills which would have been watermills driven by the Frome. But the taxable value to the king (who ranked as lord of the manor) was the then considerable sum of £73. Most of this would have come from the town at the south-western tip of Barton Regis manor. Clearly Bristow, or Bristol, was by now an important trading centre.

William II, who became king in 1087, needed to ensure the protection, and the royal domination, of the growing community. This was done under the control of Geoffrey Mowbray, Bishop of Coutances in Normandy, an active and energetic bishop as well as an important political figure and a leading landowner in England. Bishop Geoffrey supervised the building of the original Bristol Castle a short distance outside the eastern limit of the town. This was of the comparatively simple motte and bailey type, with a piled up motte, a surmounting tower, and a ditch round the base of the motte. This was towards the western end of an enclosure of some ten acres (the bailey) which would have had its own fortifications, perhaps earthworks crowned by the obstacle of timber palisades.

The Bishop of Coutances died in 1093, and the next important Norman figure in the area was Robert Fitzhamon. It was he who created a semi-independent Norman lordship in Glamorgan, started to build Cardiff Castle, and refounded Tewkesbury Abbey, to which several of Bristol's parish churches soon became appropriated. In 1106 Fitzhamon was killed in battle in Normandy. But his eldest daughter later married Robert, eventually the Earl of Gloucester, who was the ablest and the most prominent of Henry I's numerous bastard chil-

dren. Robert of Gloucester soon became the leading figure in the Bristol scene, and a man without whose consent no important local move could be made. He was also the effective ruler of Glamorgan, where in 1147, the year before his death, he founded the Cistercian abbey of Margam, near the site of Port Talbot.

Robert of Gloucester's activity in Bristol was twofold. In the castle he replaced the motte and its tower by a great quadrangular keep, of the type also seen in the Tower of London, at Rochester, and elsewhere. With dimensions of 110 feet by 95 feet, this was one of the finest late Norman keeps in England. It was built in the 1120s, and the stone-built outer fortifications of the bailey were strengthened by rectangular projecting towers, while a great hall, originally of Romanesque design, arose near the eastern end of the castle enclosure.

Robert of Gloucester also established the first of Bristol's monasteries. This was the Benedictine priory of St James, founded about 1129. It was not an independent monastery, but a 'cell' or dependency, of the Gloucesters' favourite abbey of Tewkesbury. The five western bays of its nave survive, along with the western façade with its interlaced arcading. When in 1148 Earl Robert died he was buried in the choir of St James's Priory.

Much of the reign of Stephen, who succeeded Henry I and was king from 1135 to 1154, was taken up with civil war between Stephen and his adherents and Matilda, a daughter of Henry I and at one time the Empress of the Holy Roman Empire, and her half-brother Robert of Gloucester. Bristol was a leading headquarters of the Gloucester party and its castle was briefly the prison of Stephen, captured in battle at Lincoln in 1141. Bristol was now virtually a second capital of England.

A leading Bristol townsman, who held the post of reeve, was Robert Fitzharding. In 1142 or thereabouts he founded the abbey of Augustinian canons regular, which was dedicated to St Augustine of Canterbury; a chapel of that dedication already stood to the east of the site, which was said to have been the scene of St Augustine's some-

St Augustine's Abbey (now Bristol Cathedral). Left: the Norman gateway. Above: the chapter house.

what chilly meeting with some Celtic bishops. St Augustine's became the largest, and best endowed, of the religious houses in Bristol, and was later to become Bristol's cathedral. Robert Fitzharding was the ancestor of the Earls of Berkeley. The Berkeleys, some of whom were buried in St Augustine's Abbey, remained its hereditary patrons.

In 1145 Earl Robert of Gloucester founded the preceptory of the Knights Templar, originally with an oval church, whose land included Temple Meads, now the site of Bristol's main railway station. Another associate of Earl Robert was his chamberlain, named Lewin, from whom the area known as Lewin's Mead took its name.

Out at Westbury-on-Trym – where documents prove that a church, long a dependency of the cathedral monastery at Worcester, had existed since the eighth century – a small college of secular canons was in existence from about 1194.

Stephen was succeeded, in 1154, by Henry II, the first Plantagenet king and the son of the one-time Empress Matilda by her second husband Geoffrey of Anjou. Henry is said to have spent some of his young days in Bristol, and early in his reign gave the town the first of its recorded charters. It was a short document, but gave toll-free passage, in England, Wales and Normandy; this would be of value to those who dwelt in a basically commercial community. A few years later a charter gave similar rights to those who lived in the low-lying north-ernmost area of Somerset, 'in the marsh by the bridge of Bristol'. The church of St Mary Redcliffe, originally a dependent chapel in the large parish of Bedminster, already existed in its early form and may have been started earlier in the twelfth century.

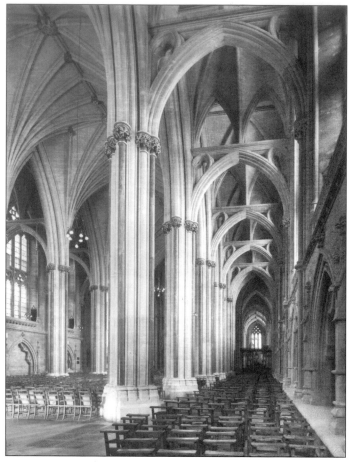

Bristol cathedral: the south aisle.

The Plantagenet kings could always rely on the loyalty of the lower Severn basin. The future King John seems to have made Bristol his semi-independent headquarters during the ten years when Richard I was king; even when he repudiated his wife (a daughter of William, Earl of Gloucester), he kept control of the town and the castle. In 1188 he issued another charter which referred to the town as a borough. As in 1155, the merchants of Bristol were guaranteed free passage throughout the kingdom, and restraints were laid on non-Bristolians, while the townsmen of Bristol were free from various feudal exactions. They could also have 'reasonable guilds'. Similar privileges to those enjoyed by Bristol were extended to various towns in Ireland, including Dublin, Waterford and Cork; close relations between Bristol and Dublin had been established early in the 1170s.

From the middle of the twelfth century Bristol became important as a centre of the wine trade, particularly with Gascony, Bordeaux on the Gironde being the chief port of shipment.

Late in the twelfth century there were developments to the south of Bristol Bridge. The church of St Mary Redcliffe was enlarged, and that of St Thomas of Canterbury, still a dependent chapel in Bedminster parish, was built shortly before 1200. The precise line of the deep-water channel of the Avon meant that there were better berthing facilities on this Somerset side of the river than on the Bristol or Gloucestershire side just below the bridge. A few houses of this period are known to have been of stone, and there was also a slip for drawing up ships in need of repair. But the greatest changes in the medieval Bristol scene awaited a spectacular undertaking in the 1240s.

Bristol's Growing Status

The death of King John in 1216 led to events in which Bristol's status was considerably enhanced. The West of England, and notably the lower valley of the Severn, became a stronghold of the Plantagenets against the invading forces of the Dauphin Louis of France. The boy king Henry III was hastily crowned by the papal legate, Cardinal Gualo, in the Abbey at Gloucester. A council was soon held in Bristol Castle, and Magna Carta was reissued under the seals of Cardinal Gualo and William Marshall, Earl of Pembroke, who was the young king's guardian. What was at issue was the assured Plantagenet succession to the throne. Henry III was at Bristol for a few months; before the end of 1216 he gave Bristol licence to choose a mayor, the first one being Adam le Page.

The first decades of the thirteenth century also saw an increase in Bristol's religious establishments. Some of Bristol's hospitals – organizations for the relief of the sick and poor – were founded in this period, in some cases by members of the Berkeley family. They included St John's Hospital close to St Mary Redcliffe, St Catherine's Hospital in Bedminster, and a hospital for leprous women near St Catherine's. A hospital for male lepers, St Lawrence's, was at Lawrence Hill on the eastern side of the town. St Bartholomew's Hospital, whose buildings eventually became those of the Grammar School, was founded by the de la Warrs. An important Berkeley benefaction, founded by Maurice le Gaunt, a grandson of Robert Fitzharding, and by his nephew Robert de Gournay, was the Hospital of St Mark, across College Green from St Augustine's Abbey. Here a hundred poor people were fed. Later run as a small religious community, this gem-like church, tucked into the College Green streetscape, is now known as the Lord Mayor's Chapel.

Bristol's first friaries were also established in the thirteenth century. That of the Dominicans, another Gaunt and Gournay foundation, was set up between 1227 and 1229. The king gave timber for the roofs from a royal forest. By 1234 the Bristol Franciscan Friary existed. It was followed by the Carmelite Friary, which was a royal foundation, while the Augustinian Friary, in the Temple Meads area, followed early in the fourteenth century; it was the only one of Bristol's four friaries built south of the Avon. The friars were supplied with fresh water by conduits from the hilly countryside close to the town.

Bristol's overseas trade included wool exports, although these never equalled those from east coast ports which had better access to the great clothmaking centres in the Low Countries. The wine trade continued to be important, employing Bristol ships (at this stage one-masted) sturdy enough to go to the Gironde and back via the Bay of Biscay. After delivering the wine in Bristol, they could return carrying as ballast lead for repairing the English king's castles in Gascony. Coarse cloth was also being produced in the area, and Bristol had also become known for its production of soft, semi-liquid, distinctly smelly soap, used for the washing of cloth rather than for personal toilet. One also hears, early in the thirteenth century, of the digging of coal in Kingswood, which in 1228 lost its status as a 'forest', though it continued as a 'chase'. Bristol ships could still be requisitioned for royal service, without payment or compensation; four 'of the best' ships were thus taken up in 1242.

The most important events in thirteenth-century Bristol were the realignment of the river harbour and the creation of what amounted to a new navigable berthing place at the new mouth of the Frome.

The Somerset side of the Avon, below the original Bristol Bridge, provided deeper water and better berthing for ships than on the Gloucestershire side. This was a matter of royal, not merely local concern. In 1239 the inhabitants on the Bristol side of the river, whose manorial lord was the king, decided to make a drastic improvement in their harbour. With the active encouragement of King Henry III, they decided to cut a new and straight channel for the lowermost reach of the Frome, which curved round the original town to enter the Avon just below the bridge. It was to run through flat, marshy ground known, from the abbey just above it, as St Augustine's Marsh. The area west of the new channel is still called Canons Marsh from the abbey's Augustinian canons. Land was bought from St Augustine's Abbey, and a new channel, about 750 yards long and at the great cost of £5000, was dug for the Frome. Much of the water of the Avon below Bristol thus flowed into the new channel, and at low tide this could have helped to drain the low-lying marshy ground between the two rivers.

The king, using the argument that the people on the Somerset, or Redcliffe, side of the Avon would benefit from the joint harbour so improved, ordered them to pay a share of the cost of the work. The new harbour was finished by 1247, and a new parish of St Stephen, including half of the Marsh and the whole of the water area of the Port of Bristol, was in due course created; most of the other area of 'The Marsh' went to that of St Nicholas. The newly created harbour at the mouth of the realigned Frome in time attracted most of Bristol's overseas shipping, while the Avon arm, with the name of the Welsh Back, became the haunt of the coasters plying each side of the Bristol Channel.

The opportunity was now taken to replace the old timber bridge with one of stone, and of four arches.

A new Bristol bridge, with houses, was built around 1250.

Houses were built on each side of this bridge, and new stretches of town wall, with semi-circular bastions in the manner of the military architecture of the thirteenth century, were put up to protect the built-up areas north of St Mary Redcliffe and between the Avon and the new channel of the Frome. A beautiful chapel, the headquarters of the religious guild of the Assumption, was built – athwart the bridge and with its own tower and spire – about a hundred years after the new bridge was finished.

In 1255, when Henry III's son, later to become Edward I, was married, various customs dues at Bristol were granted to the prince to help with the enclosure and fortification of the town. The list includes wool, hides, unshorn animal skins, sheep and goats, various kinds of fish, honey, woad, iron and lead. Carts coming in bearing saleable goods from the county of Gloucester were to pay less than those from other counties; this may allow for a toll exacted from those crossing the new Bristol bridge. Ships were to pay a higher toll than the small coasters. Similar tolls were granted, as a marriage portion, in

Gascony, Ireland, and Wales; the entire grant was administered from Bristol castle.

In the Civil War between Henry III and the forces led by Simon de Montfort, Bristol was at first on de Montfort's side. The castle held out for the king, but was eventually surrendered. The townsmen sent some ships 'of burthen' to support de Montfort, and eleven of these were lost in a naval engagement, perhaps near the mouth of the Usk, in the summer of 1265. After de Montfort's death at the battle of Evesham, Bristol was fined the large sum of £1000 for its support of the Earl of Leicester.

About the middle of the thirteenth century Bristol's first seals were cast, representing a ship under the protection of a castle or the fortifications of a defended town. These seals, representational rather than displaying the arms of the royal house or some feudal family, are the origin of the 'ship and castle' arms of the town of Bristol; later versions of the ship keep pace, eventually with cannon, with later developments in the hull design and rig of the maritime element in these famous arms.

By the end of the thirteenth century Bristol had its Members of the House of Commons as well as its mayors; John le Taverner is the first Member of Parliament whose name is recorded.

The fourteenth century was notable in Bristol for the growth of a high-quality cloth industry, replacing and enhancing the rough cloth already made in the town. The cloth trade was long concentrated south of the Avon, in the district near Temple Church. The weavers, who were also linked to the tuckers and dyers, were members of a guild which had a chapel in the Temple Church. When the Knights Templar were suppressed the church became a parish church under the name of Holy Cross. The chapel of the weavers' guild continued, but the famous leaning tower of Temple Church was of later dates and in the Perpendicular style.

The early years of the century, notably the short period from 1314 to 1316 when Edward II was king, were marked by what amounted to a rebellion by Bristol against the authority of the king and his officers. A leading figure in the movement against the king was John le Taverner, who had already been the town's mayor and one of its Members of Parliament. There was a riot round the Guildhall, with some deaths, and in 1316 a royal army, and a blockading fleet, took action against the rebellious town. In July 1316 the town gave in and was heavily fined.

The Great Dungeon Tower, Bristol Castle, from Millerd's plan of 1673.

In 1317 the king was given a three years' grant of local tolls and customs receipts to pave the town and repair damage done, on its eastern side, in the bombardment from the castle.

The range of goods coming in was now wider. Wine, corn, hides and skins (including those of cats and squirrels) are listed, also cloth, linen, canvas, and various luxury textiles. Fish, vegetables, salt, cheese, and butter are likewise mentioned, also coal, nails and other metal goods, dried fish (stockfish), herrings, hemp and oil. Woad is also mentioned for the dyeing of white or off-white cloth.

The making and export of high-grade cloth continued in fourteenth-century Bristol, with helpful expertise perhaps coming from the Belgian part of the Low Countries, from which Edward III took his young queen. From 1344 onwards the mayor and the chief officials of the town were supported by a town council.

The craft or trade guilds continued their activities. Their rules, along with the charters of other towns and regulations for the government of Bristol itself, were set down by the Recorder in a volume of 1344 known, from its binding of red-deer skin, as 'The Little Red Book'. Seventeen trade guilds had their rules recorded. In addition there were the guilds, or religious societies, with a mainly devotional purpose.

Bristol was still liable to send ships to form the fleets when the king was engaged in warlike operations. In 1346 a large fleet was gathered for the transport of men and supplies to Calais. Bristol's contribution came to 24 ships manned by 608 men. The figure was about the same as that for London, but much greater than those of other ports on the Bristol Channel.

A particularly severe attack of bubonic plague, known as the Black Death, hit Bristol in 1348, and about a third of the population are believed to have died. The rebuilding of St Mary Recliffe had started before the plague, in the 1340s, but it was eventually continued, with the rare features for a parish church of doubly aisled transepts and an eastern Lady Chapel, in the Perpendicular rather than the Decorated style. The work may have been finished by about 1400.

The French wars continued at intervals, and the Spaniards, too, were sometimes enemies. In 1372 a disastrous action off La Rochelle against a French and Spanish fleet caused the loss of at least eleven ships from Bristol. Important events in the next year could have come as some compensation for this serious blow.

The townsmen of Bristol petitioned the elderly king Edward III for a charter, which was granted, and which was of particular benefit to the members of the merchant community. The town, so far divided between Gloucestershire and Somerset, was made a small county in its own right. This charter was granted at Woodstock on 8 August 1373. Later documents appointed commissioners to determine the exact boundaries of the new county and set out the geographical details. For church purposes Bristol was still divided between the bishoprics of Worcester and Bath and Wells.

Assizes were to be held in Bristol itself, and the sheriff of the new county was to be appointed from among the local merchants and not from the landed gentry of Gloucestershire or Somerset. Bristol townsmen involved in lawsuits at the assizes were no longer to make the journey to Gloucester or the sometimes dangerous and muddy excursion to the low-lying, marsh-girt town of Ilchester. Such journeys, allowing for two days each way and time spent on legal proceedings, could keep a Bristol merchant from his business for at least a week, with expenses on the journey and at the seat of justice. A town gaol was to be set up in Bristol itself, so avoiding the need, and expense, of conveying local prisoners to Gloucestershire or Somerset prisons.

The new mayor was to be sworn in each year. The Charter refers to the good disposition of Bristol to the crown, and to the good service of the townsmen. Apart from other expenses a fee of 600 marks (£400) had to be paid for the Charter; the arms of the king, and of Bristol, are included in the fancifully illuminated documents. The main one dated 8 August 1373 includes a portrait miniature of the elderly king, armed and robed with a crown on his head. He is shown with white hair and a forked beard, which corresponds with the beard shown on his bronze effigy in Westminster Abbey.

Two later documents, even richer in fanciful illumination, date from 30 October and 20 December 1373. In one, outlining the proposed boundaries of the small new county, Edward III is depicted wearing an ermine cape, an ermine-lined cloak and a splendid robe adorned out with the fleurs-de-lis of France. The other document, in which the initial letters of some Latin sentences are picked out in gold or blue, bears a more striking miniature. The king is shown seated on a throne clad in a long blue robe; he holds a sceptre in one hand, but no orb.

It has been said that Bristol's High Cross (now at Stourhead, Wiltshire) was put up to commemorate the town's new status. It seems likely that it was erected about fifty years later.

Bristol's population was now spreading, across the Frome and in the area of Broadmead, beyond such parishes as those of St John the Baptist and St Lawrence. So in 1374 five bays of the nave of the Benedictine Priory of St James were turned into a parish church; a new roof, supported on corbels of this period, was added at the same time, and a tower was put up to hold the parishioners' bells.

In 1377 a poll tax was levied. The clergy were separately reckoned, and friars and children were omitted. The figure given for Bristol is 6345, so the entire population could have been a little over 10,000. London paid the tax on over 23,000 people, while York is the only provincial town to exceed the numbers given for Bristol.

The Canynges and the Cabots

In the later Middle Ages, from 1400 onwards, Bristol's life continued to be overwhelmingly mercantile, with the leading merchants putting money into houses – for the most part timber-framed but with party walls and some other details of stone. The castle, with its great Norman keep and one turret rising higher than the other three, still had its constables, but as it was a royal domain it remained a part of Gloucestershire and was excluded from the new Bristol county arrangements of 1373. Henry VI visited Bristol in 1446, although he was more occupied with his plans for his colleges at Eton and Cambridge than with the affairs of a provincial trading town. Edward IV's visit, fifteen years later, was of greater note for Bristol. On that occasion Sir Baldwin Fulford, a Lancastrian knight from Devon, was executed. The younger William Canynges, who figures prominently later in this book, was serving one of his periods as mayor at the time. The general sympathies of the Bristol merchants seem to have been Yorkist.

Bristol's trade continued much as before, with cloth going out to Gascony. The French kings were steadily eating into the English holding in Guienne. They took Bordeaux in 1451 and the last remnants of the English-held province collapsed after Talbot's defeat in 1453. This defeat brought the wine trade with the Gironde to a halt for a few years. Wine came in from Spain and Portugal, and dried fruit from Spain and the Mediterranean, along with the well-tried imports of hides, woad, and other dyestuffs. The voyages to southern Spain and Portugal, involving a fairly long run into the eastern reaches of the Atlantic, were significant for Bristol's maritime future.

The last decades of the fourteenth century, and well into the fifteenth, were notable for the important role played by successive generations of the Canynges family; they may well have come from the parishes, near Devizes in Wiltshire, of All Cannings or Bishop's Cannings. The first John Canynges appears in Bristol in the 1330s and 1340s. The elder William was prominent in Bristol as a merchant, as the town's mayor on four occasions, and as its Member of Parliament for three sessions. He died in 1396. The second John Canynges, who died in 1405, was a clothier and a merchant who traded abroad. Like other members of the family, he lived in the parish of St Thomas, which still counted as a dependent chapel in the parish of Bedminster. But his activities, and his public life, would have often taken him into the other (once Gloucestershire) part of Bristol. One of his sons, another William, was the best-known member of the family, as a shipowner, a leading figure in Bristol's civic life, Member of Parliament, and eventually as a priest.

The second William Canynges was not in the cloth trade himself, but he was the owner of several ships which carried cloth and other Bristol exports. We have valuable details from the topographical writer and surveyor of buildings, William Worcestre. Nine ships are named, and one other is said to have been lost off Iceland. One, which had cost about £2600, was named the *Mary and John* and is said to have been of about 900 tons, an extremely large ship for that time; it is likely to have had three masts rather than the single mast of earlier medieval ships using the port of Bristol. Another, named the *Mary Redcliffe*, was of 500 tons. Canynges is said to have employed eight hundred men as the crews of his ships, and he also employed a hundred men as workmen, and as carpenters, masons and in other trades.

Though he lived near St Thomas's church, Canynges was also concerned with the more impressive building of St Mary Redcliffe. He founded two chantries there, and in the south transept one sees the canopied tomb with two effigies of Canynges and his wife Joan, probably erected well before Joan Canynges' death in 1467.

William Canynges the younger may well have expected the death of his wife, and he seems already, as a pious man, to have planned to enter the priesthood, which he could do only as a widower. He was aided in his intentions by John Carpenter, who was from 1444 to 1476 the Bishop of Worcester and therefore had the college at Westbury-on-Trym in his diocese. He was not, however, responsible for St Thomas's or St Mary Redcliffe, in whose area Canynges had his home and where the tomb showing him as a civilian originated in the first and longest phase of Canynges' career.

Bishop Carpenter, who had been a leading figure at Oxford, Chancellor of the University and Provost of Oriel, quickly saw him through all the stages of ordination, from acolyte in 1467 to priest in 1468. In 1469 Canynges became dean of the small college at Westbury which was rebuilt at this time. He continued as dean until his death in 1474, probably in his early seventies. His second effigy, in alabaster, showing him in the choir habit of a priest, is now in St Mary Redcliffe but could have been moved there from the church at Westbury.

Bristol was not much concerned in the Wars of the Roses, though Margaret of Anjou passed through the town, and may have been welcomed there, in 1471, on her way to the Lancastrian defeat at Tewkesbury and the execution of her son Prince Edward. Some of those who must, perhaps reluctantly, have welcomed her were fined or briefly imprisoned. A few years later we have the vivid picture in the 1479 'Calendar' of the Town Clerk Robert Ricart of the swearing in of a mayor, before his predeces-

The swearing-in ceremony of the Mayor of Bristol, from Ricart's Calendar, 1479.

sor, as laid down in the Charter of 1373. The ceremony took place in the Guild Hall, and shows the arms of Bristol, the royal arms of England as they then were, and St George's Cross on a white ground. One of Bristol's splendid collection of civic swords is shown in the picture, borne by a swordbearer. Ricart was a member of the Fraternity, or Guild, of Calendars, with its headquarters in All Saints' Church. Its members were priests, scriveners and others whose work involved the compilation and keeping of records.

Bristol's overseas trade was still mainly with the wine-producing areas of south-western France and Spain and Portugal. To avoid a long overland journey, some pilgrims travelled from Bristol by ship to the shrine, in north-western Spain, of Santiago de Compostela. Few ships from Bristol ventured far into the Mediterranean; goods from that area were more likely to be freighted on the large Venetian or Genoese carracks, to be landed on the south coast and brought overland by pack-horses, if they were destined for Bristol. But one Bristol merchant, Robert Sturmy, who was mayor in 1453–4, did get a licence to trade in wool, tin, lead and cloth, to visit Pisa, and to carry pilgrims to Jerusalem. This was in 1446, and the outward voyage was successful. But on the return voyage they encountered strong northerly winds, and were wrecked with the loss of thirty-seven men. In 1457 Sturmy was encouraged to make another voyage deep into the Mediterranean. He was intercepted and plundered by Genoese ships. In retaliation Genoese citizens in England were detained till Sturmy was compensated from their property.

Voyages continued to be made to Spain, Portugal, and their Atlantic islands, mainly for wine but also for small quantities of sugar, which was now produced both in southern Spain and in Madeira. A few voyages, with cloth in return for fish dried in the chilly wind, were made to Iceland, and when Columbus visited 'Island' he found that Bristol merchants were predominant among foreign traders in goods normally supposed to go through the Danish kings' 'staple' at Bergen which was, at that time, under Danish rule.

The fifteenth century is noteworthy for the detailed accounts handed down by William Worcestre, a pioneer in English topographical writing. He was a land surveyor by occupation and training and was for some years the business manager of Sir John Falstaff of Caister Castle in Norfolk. Born in Bristol, about 1415, Worcestre came of a burgess family; his uncle was a priest. His mother, who came from Coventry and from a well-to-do family, was called Elizabeth Botoner, and he normally used her surname rather than that of Worcestre. Eventually he lived in Bristol, in a house in the parish of Saints Philip and James the Less.

His *Itinerarium* covers many places as well as Bristol, and is of special value for the dimensions given of many buildings, including abbey churches, which have since been destroyed. William's records, which include the list of the younger William Canynges' ships, give details, including measurements, of surviving churches such as St Mary Redcliffe and of friary churches which were destroyed at the Reformation. He also, with a land surveyor's professional interest, mentions the length and breadth of streets and alleys, and such mundane details as public lavatories and stairs or slip-ways over the tidal mud that enabled women to wash clothes, at low tide, in the water of the Avon.

He mentions the merchant Robert Sturmy, pays tribute to his lavish hospitality, and records the disaster of 1446 when Sturmy's ship was wrecked on the southern coast of the Peloponnese in Greece. The manuscript volume, now in the library of Corpus Christi College at Cambridge, is scrappy and haphazardly arranged. William may have meant to arrange it more systematically, before its publication; some is in Latin, some in English. Wedged between other details of Bristol in the fifteenth century are references to an Atlantic voyage made by a brother-in-law of William Worcestre.

The navigator was the younger John Jay, who made his voyage in 1480, and laid down his brass, perhaps in the expectation of failure and fatal shipwreck, in St Mary Redcliffe. The date of Jay's departure from Kingroad (the stretch of water between the mouth of the Avon and Portishead) was 15 July 1480, and he came back to the

Avon in September of the same year. But we do not know the exact dates of his death or that of his wife, Joan. The navigational information given by William Worcestre's account is of great interest as part of a maritime story which culminated in 1497.

Jay's ship was small – of only eighty tons – but may have been a three-masted caravel. His objective, far to the west of Ireland, was the supposed Isle of Brasylle or 'Brasile', where it was reckoned supplies of brazilletto wood could be obtained. Fragments of this wood (actually from Central America rather than what later became known as Brazil) may have reached European waters carried on the Gulf Stream. Ground up, brazilletto wood could be used to produce a reddish-brown cloth dye. A successful voyage would be of value to cloth-makers in Bristol and the West of England. So Jay, with the aid of a pilot whose name seems to have been Llyde or Lloyd, and who ranked as one of the most skilled and experienced mariners in England, set out from the port of Bristol, furrowing the Atlantic for about nine weeks. They found no island of the type they sought, but were driven back by bad weather and eventually made a port in Ireland where they could repair the ship and victual the crew.

In the summer of 1481 two more Bristol ships sailed out on the same search, inevitably fruitless, for Brazil. Eleven years later Columbus, mistakenly hoping that he would, after a voyage of no more than three thousand miles, arrive at the Spice Islands in the East Indies, crossed the Atlantic and arrived in the Bahamas. Later voyages took him to the more extensive islands of the West Indies and to within sight of the mainland of Central America. Here was a vast new land mass, soon divided, by a Papal award and by a treaty in 1493 and 1494, between Spain and Portugal; the division of the globe could, in theory, run as far as the North and South Poles; Florida and southern Chile were in fact the limits of Iberian settlement.

It was soon most doubtful that Columbus's discoveries could be any part of Cathay (Japan) or the Spice Islands.

There remained the quest for Brazil, and for the Isle of the Seven Cities, said to exist somewhere in the Atlantic. England, and in particular Bristol with its expertise in deep-sea navigation, became involved in this search, and John Cabot was the seaman who actually, in the summer of 1497, crossed the North Atlantic and made a brief landing. His venture came as a sequel to events in Bristol which involved Henry VII, the first Tudor king.

Henry visited Bristol in 1486, the year after he gained the throne. He was there again in 1490, seeking the support of the mercantile and trading class. Atlantic probings had continued from Bristol since Jay's venture of 1480. Henry probably discussed the idea that such voyages could profitably be made to Brasile and the Seven Cities and – in these years before Columbus' somewhat unpromising discoveries of 1492 and 1493 – in search of Cathay or the spice-bearing Moluccas. Any voyages from an English port would, of course, have to be made well to the north of Brazil, which was allocated to Portugal, and well clear of the Spanish islands such as Cuba, Santo Domingo, and Puerto Rico. Bristol provided much of the backing for the momentous voyage of which the prime mover was, like Columbus, from Italy.

John Cabot (more correctly, Giovanni Caboto) was of Italian birth, and in 1476 became a citizen of Venice. He was an expert seaman, making journeys to Egypt and also to Mecca, in the hope of buying spices which had come by sea passage across the Indian Ocean and then by caravans. But a voyage across the Atlantic could, in theory, reach the Spice Islands by a back-door approach. Columbus, unaware of the distance across the American continent and then through the Pacific, had worked on this idea, and the climate of the West Indies seemed to correspond to that of what is now known as Indonesia. But Columbus's voyages had been under the patronage of the Spanish Crown. Cabot was almost certainly in Spain in 1493, and he may have met Bristol merchants there. By the

A portrait (c. 1500) of Henry VII, who commissioned John Cabot to find a new sea route to the riches of the east.

Cabot Tower on Brandon Hill, erected in 1897 to mark the 400th anniversary of the momentous voyage of discovery.

end of 1495 he was in Bristol and in contact with the merchants of the port most likely to contain expertise in Atlantic navigation. He also had important planning discussions with Henry VII in London.

In March 1496 the king granted Letters Patent to John Cabot and his sons Lodovico, Sebastiano and Sanzio to cross the Atlantic, not far enough south to clash with areas of Spanish occupation (and thereby incur the displeasure of Ferdinand and Isabella, whose daughter, Catherine,

Henry was hoping to marry to his eldest son, Arthur). They were to run west along the approximate latitude of Bristol, and if they came to lands 'unknown to Christians', and hence well north of the West Indies and Central America, they were to 'conquer, occupy, and possess' them – including any towns and castles they might encounter – in the name of the English Crown. They were also to spread Christianity among any people they might

18

meet. They might take five ships, with as many men as Cabot and his sons might think fit. The ships and their equipment were to be provided by Cabot and the Bristol patrons, but a fifth of any trading profit was to go to the king.

A Spanish account of Cabot's voyages strongly indicates that there was a first voyage, by only one ship, in the summer of 1496. No traces of land were found. The wind was contrary, food ran short and the discontented crew insisted on returning. Cabot therefore waited till the late spring of 1497. He set out, again taking just one ship – a small three-masted caravel called the *Matthew* – with a crew of only eighteen or twenty men; the Bristol merchants were probably cautious and experimental in their approach. They left port on or just before 20 May. Their last European land fall was Dursey Head in south-western Ireland. The ship made reasonably steady progress against some contrary winds, and on 24 June – Midsummer's Day, when there would be long daylight – John Cabot and his crew sighted land, probably near the northern tip of Newfoundland. It was also a few miles from the temporary settling place, about five hundred years earlier, of Norsemen from Greenland.

Cabot and some of his men went ashore. In accordance with the king's Letters Patent they set up a banner with the Royal Arms of England, and also a crucifix and the arms of Pope Alexander VI. They soon found, from an extinguished camp fire and other traces, including a stick painted with red ochre which they took to be from brazilletto wood, that the land was inhabited, so they did not dare to venture far inland. They found good grass which seemed promising for cattle pastures. They also found pine woods from which masts and spars could be made. They coasted down the eastern side of Newfoundland, and across the Cabot Strait to Cape Breton Island at the northern tip of Nova Scotia.

On their way they sailed across the Grand Banks and there, in shallow water, came across vast quantities of cod, the fishing of which soon became the main economic asset of Newfoundland. When they coasted down Nova Scotia (perhaps as far south as the level of Halifax) they would have seen part of the mainland of North America, but a landing in Cape Breton Island, or anywhere else in Nova Scotia, is less likely than one on the Newfoundland coast.

Finally, after a quick homeward passage of only fifteen days, they reached Bristol, where their friends would have been pleased at the firm evidence of softwood timber and of cod, and at the possibility of brazilletto wood. Cabot was soon in London, much lionised, and when he saw the king he was given an immediate grant of £10, with a pension of £20 a year, the money being found from the customs revenue of Bristol. John Cabot left no personal record of his voyage, but he saw a Venetian in London named Pasqualigo, also Soncino, the Milanese ambassador whose long account is the nearest we have to an eye witness record.

Later in 1497 Henry VII was preoccupied with the aftermath of Perkin Warbeck's rebellion. He levied fines on many in the West of England who had supported Warbeck. He was at Exeter for a month, but back in London later in the year for talks with Cabot about a second voyage. With the Spanish ambassador he had delicate discussions concerning Cabot's first voyage and another planned for 1498, and the intended marriage between the young Catherine of Aragon and the Prince of Wales.

John Cabot was still based in Bristol, gathering money, provisions, and other supplies for a second expedition across the Atlantic. In February of 1498, he got Letters Patent which formally permitted this second voyage. This was with five ships, one a royal vessel, the others provided by London and Bristol merchants. Enough men were sent to found a trading station. Two priests were among the crews, and barter goods were shipped to help trade with transatlantic inhabitants. The little squadron assembled at Bristol and left there late in May or early in June. One ship came back, in a damaged state, to a port in Ireland. Nothing more was heard of the rest, and it is generally assumed that Cabot perished on the voyage, at sea or in some disastrous encounter with the Indians or, exploring further south, with Spanish pirates. Another school of thought suggests, tantalisingly, that Cabot in fact returned safely and embarked on further voyages in the coming years. The truth will probably never be known.

A few years later some Bristol merchants, who may have been looking for a sea passage to the north of the newly found continent, secured Letters Patent allowing them, and some Portuguese sailors from the Azores, to sail without restriction to all lands discovered over the Atlantic.

Sebastian Cabot, who was granted an annual pension of £10 in 1505, emerges as the next transatlantic venturer from Bristol. By 1509 it was realised that the American continent, and then the wide ocean of the Pacific, lay between Europe and Cathay or the Spice Islands. To reach the Pacific a sea passage, north or south of the Americas, had to be discovered. International politics made a north-west passage the safer option. Early in 1509 Sebastian Cabot left Bristol with two ships, large enough to carry considerable crews. They reached Newfoundland or Labrador, coasted north and seem likely to have sailed through the Hudson Strait and into the beginnings of Hudson's Bay and then south down the bay's eastern side. There seemed no promise, here to the north of what later became known as Canada, of a passage to the Pacific or Cathay.

Discouraged by the severe conditions, the Bristol men in the ships' crews insisted on a return home. But first of all Sebastian coasted, in the hope of finding a promising inlet, far down the eastern seaboard of what is now the United States. Later in the year he sailed back to Bristol, to find that Henry VII was dead. Henry VIII was more interested in the politics of the continent of Europe than in

Sebastian Cabot, who survived his father to explore the North American coastline.

ventures across the Atlantic. Bristol settled down to its well-established trading pattern of woollen cloth for wine.

Life under Henry VIII and Elizabeth

After the return of Sebastian Cabot, to an England with Henry VIII on the throne, Bristol's trade continued much as before, with fresh families prominent in the town's business life. These included Robert and Nicholas Thorne and Thorne's son, also named Robert, who lived in Seville and supervised the Spanish end of the family business; Spanish wine, and possibly some sugar, would have been among the commodities he sent to Bristol. In the meantime, and before the important changes of the Reformation, a new educational foundation came into being.

About 1532 the buildings of St Bartholomew's Hospital, across the River Frome from the central part of the town, were converted into Bristol's Grammar School, founded by the Thorne family. The school, which would remain on this low-lying site for over two centuries, was meant to provide nautical and commercial education for a literate and scientifically equipped merchant class. Nicholas Thorne left the new foundation his astrolabe and some other scientific instruments. The hospital buildings, and some suburban landed property, were made over to the City corporation, whose members were to be the school's future governors.

Around this time events in national politics made for great changes in the Bristol religious scene. In 1534 Parliament declared Henry VIII Supreme Head of the Church in England. At first, parish churches were not affected, but the religious houses, in Bristol and elsewhere, saw drastic change. The friaries were suppressed and their sites were sold to various lay owners. A fine Tudor mansion, the property of Sir John Young, soon arose on the site of the Carmelite Friary, while William Chester obtained the Dominican site. St Augustine's Abbey was dissolved, in 1539, among the greater monasteries, and the tiny St Mary Magdalene's Priory was also suppressed. Its buildings, near the bottom of St Michael's Hill, could never have been extensive, but the name survives in the present Maudlin Street. St James's Priory, being a dependency of the Abbey at Tewkesbury, awaited the dissolution of that great Benedictine abbey in 1540.

The hospitals, run on quasi-monastic lines by religious brethren, were also dissolved. In Bristol, these included St Mark's, or the Gaunt's Hospital, whose church was soon made over to the Corporation and is now, after various restoration works, widely known as the Lord Mayor's Chapel, one of the very few churches in England which belongs to a municipality. Dr Owen, a physician at court, received the grant of St John's Hospital near St Mary Redcliffe. Other almshouses, though run under religious auspices and with secular clergy as their chaplains, continued their charitable work.

The most important development in Bristol under Henry VIII was the creation of its bishopric; from now onwards Bristol could call itself a city. Now that the king had, in England, replaced the Pope he could create new bishoprics, using abbey churches as the cathedrals of the new sees. These were: Peterborough; Chester, which then covered Lancashire as well as Cheshire; Westminster, for the tenure of only one bishop; Oxford; Gloucester, with its cathedral in St Peter's Abbey, and including Gloucestershire east of the Severn; and Bristol. The new Bristol diocese was based on a town whose population was by now about 11,000, the largest in England without a bishopric. Its boundaries were unusual; they included the city of Bristol, a few parishes at the southern end of Gloucestershire, and the county of Dorset, which was taken from Salisbury, and whose inclusion in the diocese of Bristol meant that the new diocese was in two separate portions.

For its cathedral the new diocese had the abbey church of St Augustine. The nave may already have been pulled down, or was in such a poor condition that its demolition was inevitable. So Bristol Cathedral was, along with that of Oxford, a small cathedral, consisting only of its architecturally important choir limb, its transepts, and the central tower above its crossing. It recalled such T-shaped college chapels as those of New College, Magdalen, and All Souls' at Oxford. No longer a monastic church of Canons Regular it became, like such other cathedrals as those of Wells, Exeter, and Salisbury, a collegiate church served by secular clergy; hence the name 'College Green' applied to the space on one side of the cathedral both here and at Gloucester.

Compared to some other ancient bishoprics the new see of Bristol was very poorly endowed; the same applied to the income of its deanery. Half the income of St Augustine's Abbey went to finance the new bishopric. Other revenues were added, but the income of the Bristol see was so small that in Elizabeth I's reign the diocese was sometimes held jointly with that of Gloucester. The deanery was endowed with some remaining revenues of St Augustine's, along with some pickings from such West of England abbeys as Shaftesbury, Bruton and Muchelney. A cathedral grammar school, replacing some sort of a school run by the canons of St Augustine's, is now the Cathedral School; it was mainly concerned with the education of the choristers but some other boys came in 'to learn grammar'.

The first Bishop of Bristol was Paul Bush, once Prior of the 'Bonshommes' at Edington in Wiltshire, who followed the Rule of St Augustine. The first dean of the newly elevated cathedral was another one-time Augustinian canon, William Snow, who had been Prior of Bradenstoke between Chippenham and Swindon. Paul Bush remained bishop till Mary I's accession in 1553.

The 1549 Prayer Book of Edward VI's reign caused trouble and rebellion in Devon and Cornwall, but neither there nor elsewhere did it have much effect on the furnishing of the churches. The much more Protestant Prayer Book of 1552 had more drastic results. The chantries had by now been abolished, with severe effects on the fittings and furnishings of many aisles or side chapels. It was now the turn of the rood screens, the lofts which supported the crucifixion groups, and the sanctuaries with their high altars of stone. These altars made way, in each church, for a plain wooden communion table. The chancels lay open to the naves without screens, but perhaps with low partitions. Mass vestments were abolished, as were banners and statues, while wall paintings, where they were not ruthlessly destroyed, were whitewashed over, the whitewash coming in handy as a background for scriptural texts for the minority who could read them.

The devastation extended, on a massive scale, to the rich accumulation of church plate, particularly altar ornaments and Mass plate. Chalices were almost all destroyed, and sent to the Bristol Mint for melting down. Each church could keep only one chalice for the comparatively rare celebrations of Holy Communion. Very few examples remain in Bristol of the pre-Reformation apparatus of worship. Two pairs of Limoges enamel altar candlesticks survive from the original church of St Thomas. This church was re-dedicated under Henry VIII, who disliked the memory of Becket (as one who had stood up to a king), to St Thomas the Apostle. The fine brass eagle lectern, originally in St Nicholas's but now in St Stephen's and perhaps from Flanders, survived because it was still useful for reading the lessons at morning and evening prayer. The splendid brass chandelier, of the fifteenth century and originally in the church of the Holy Cross, Temple is now in the Cathedral.

The Bristol Mint, of which Sir William Sharington, by now the owner of Lacock Abbey, was Treasurer, received much of the church plate for melting down and converting into coin. Sharington was soon accused of putting too little silver into these coins and keeping the balance of the metal for himself. He was dismissed, and only his death in 1553 prevented his trial on what would have been a capital charge.

Another event of 1552 concerned the regulation of Bristol's trade. The Society of Merchant Venturers, which may have grown out of earlier fellowships of merchants, formally came into being on 18 December. It received its grant of arms, adapted from those of the Merchant Adventurers of London, in 1569, on the same day that the Heralds granted augmentations to the arms of the City of Bristol.

The reign of Mary I, from 1553 to 1558, included the restoration of the Mass and the refitting, so far as this was possible, of the parish churches. Great activity and considerable expense occurred when the churches were refurnished for Catholic worship; some of the new fittings could, in the 1550s, have included elements of Renaissance design. At Christ Church £10 was spent on a new rood loft; this would have been the most conspicuous item of refurnishing. Stone altars were reinstated, but there was no revival of the chantries. Mary's reign saw the execution of extreme Protestants in Bristol. Five almost certainly suffered in this way, and there may have been a few more, all of them craftsmen from humble stations of life. There were many more burnings in the London area. Of the bishops who died in Mary I's reign Latimer had been at Worcester, and in that capacity had preached Reformed doctrines at the Bristol end of his diocese; this was in the 1530s, before the creation of the new Bristol bishopric.

In Elizabeth's I's reign Bristol's trade with Spain and Portugal continued while there was still formal peace

Queen Elizabeth I enters the city through St John's arch on her 1574 visit.

with Spain, though the volume of this business, in cloth and Mendip lead, seems to have declined gradually. Bristol merchants, some from newly leading families such as the Aldworths, Kitchens and Whitsons, could still reside, with no problems of religious differences, in Spanish ports. But increasing trouble with Spain, although still short of open war, meant that Bristol's trade was increasingly precarious. It must have come as a tonic when Elizabeth I herself ceremoniously visited Bristol in August 1574 as part of one of her 'progresses', which continued almost to the end of her life. In the earlier part of her reign these progresses were 'politically directed' to areas where woollen manufactures flourished; a visit to Norfolk, including Norwich, occurred in 1578.

The queen arrived from the direction of Berkeley, and was met at Lawford's Gate. In the middle of the city the High Cross was freshly painted and gilded in honour of the royal visitor. She stayed, for the few days of her visit, in John Young's comparatively new 'Great House' on the site of the Carmelite friary. Young was knighted as a reward for putting his house at Elizabeth's disposal; four other knights were created at the same time. On the Sunday of her visit the queen attended service in the cathedral. She may also have noticed the architectural magnificence of St Mary Redcliffe, for she is on record as saying that it was 'the fairest, goodliest and most famous parish [as distinct from cathedral or one-time monastic] church in England'.

Elizabeth's entertainment in Bristol included a strong element of oratory as well as formal reception by the mayor and other dignitaries. She was greeted by orations, composed for them by a man named Churchyard, by boys named, for this royal occasion, Fame (who greeted the queen at the High Cross), Salutation, Gratulation, and Obedient Good Will.

Some state business had to be conducted while the queen was in Bristol. The commissioners responsible for drafting a trade treaty with the King of Spain caught up with her here. Although known as the Treaty of Bristol, this was of more concern to London merchants than those of Bristol, and addressed problems over the Spanish Netherlands.

The more spectacular aspect of Elizabeth I's Bristol visit concerned mock naval activity in the river harbour, including a sham fight just below the junction of the Avon and Frome. There were more formal speeches and the queen gave a large sum of money to provide the soldiers who fought the mock battles with a lavish banquet; they also lowered six barrels of beer and six dozen bottles of ale. She left Bristol, for Wilton near Salisbury, 'marvel-lously contented' with what she had seen. The city of Bristol had spent over £1000 on the visit. More than half of this came from a 'general collection' from the inhabitants, while £450 was borrowed from the charity funds.

In 1575 there was a serious outbreak of plague in Bristol; one of the victims was John Cutte, who had been mayor in 1566–7. The city, as one sees from a map of 1580, had not yet expanded much. This map, by a German mapmaker named Hoefnagle, appeared in an atlas portraying the chief towns of the world. Geographically speaking, it is reasonably correct, but it has no claim to architectural accuracy in the buildings it depicts. The castle has no dominating Norman keep, and the cathedral, shown as a building still with a nave, is marked as 'Great St Augustine's'. Bristol, or Brightstowe, is described as the 'florentissimum Angliae emporium', and three figures, two men and a woman, in early Elizabethan costume, stand in the foreground of what is a 'perspective view' rather than a two-dimensional map of the modern type.

The castle, which was still royal property and whose constable was the Earl of Pembroke, was used in the 1560s for experiments in brass-making by a chartered company known as the Mineral and Battery Works, in which the earl was a shareholder. Copper ore came by sea from Cornwall, calamine was dug in the Mendips, and local coal from Kingswood was used in the smelting process. One purpose of the work was the production of brass for the casting of bronze cannon; these could be most useful if privateering expeditions made way for open war against Spain. For Bristol this work was a start on the city's long, and important, history of coal-fired industry; pinmaking, with the use of brass wire, became important in the seven-teenth century.

A famous Bristol school was established in the 1580s, from an endowment by John Carr, a local soapmaker, modelled on Christ's Hospital in London, including the long dark-blue gowns resembling the church costume of that time. The school, housed in the Gaunts' Hospital, opened with twelve pupils in 1590, when a charter provided that it should be called Queen Elizabeth's Hospital.

The year 1588 had been that of the Armada. Four Bristol ships had sailed to Plymouth, not to take part in the fighting, whose brunt was borne by the queen's low-built, efficient galleons, but to form part of the 'Fleet train' which kept the fighting vessels supplied. Canvas bought and stored in Bristol was sent to make tents in the camp at Tilbury. The Armada was beaten and dispersed, but the drying up of the export of cloth caused distress and depri-vation in Bristol and elsewhere in the western counties. Only peace with Spain, made by James VI in the first year of his reign, could open the way to more prosperous times both for the clothiers and those whose concern was more specifically with imports from the Iberian peninsula. These were the members of the Spanish Company, of London and Bristol alike, one of whose members added to the total of Bristol's endowed schools by establishing a school for girls.

More Voyages of Discovery

Since the Cabots' time there had been no transatlantic ventures from the port of Bristol. But the idea of some English-speaking Protestant settlement in the Americas was kept alive, disastrously so when Raleigh founded his short-lived settlement in what is now North Carolina, in 'Virginia'. (This name – a tribute to the Virgin Queen, Elizabeth I – applied to a long stretch of the eastern seaboard.) The settlement lasted less than a year.

An active advocate of such voyages, which had as their purpose permanent settlement, was the younger Richard Hakluyt. From 1585 he held a canonry in Bristol Cathedral and was thus partly resident in the city, where he could expound his ideas to leading local merchants. The first actual ventures of Bristolians to what eventually became known as New England occurred soon after the turn of the century.

In 1602 some Bristol seamen were in the crew of Captain Bartholomew Gosnold, who sailed to the coast of what is now Maine and brought back some sassafras, which was valued as a medicinal herb. The following year a voyage backed by the Bristol merchants John Whitson and Robert Aldworth, with Martin Pring in charge of the ship, left Bristol five days before the death of Elizabeth I. Their American landfall was in Maine, but they sailed south to a more promising harbour, which they called Whitson Harbour, giving the name Mount Aldworth to a neighbouring hill. The bay itself had the name Plymouth Harbour by 1616; it later became famous as the landing place, in 1620, of the Pilgrim Fathers. As it was early in the summer, the venturers of 1603 sowed seeds of such familiar crops as wheat, barley, oats, leeks, and onions. Before

John Whitson: a Bristol merchant who financed an expedition to the Americas, served as the city's mayor and MP, and founded the Red Maids' School.

the end of the summer they flourished, and the settlers were satisfied that the soil was suitable for cultivation.

A few years later, in 1606, two more ships left Bristol for North Virginia, under the overall command of Martin Pring. The chief sponsors were Sir Ferdinando Gorges of Wraxall near Bristol and Lord Chief Justice Popham, who had been Bristol's Recorder. One ship was taken by the Spaniards, but the other reached New England, where the crew made a detailed reconnaissance of the coast. Another ship, sent out by Popham in 1607, carried emigrants and supplies for a permanent colony. But the governor of the little colony died, many stores were lost in a fire, and the severity of the New England winter was far worse than had been expected after the reasonably mild summer. So the disillusioned colonists came home, and Bristol's involvement in American settlement was interrupted for a few years.

It was now the turn of permanent on-shore settlement in Newfoundland to form a base for those who went to exploit the cod fisheries. An initial 'plantation' was established in 1610 by a prominent Bristolian named John Guy; apart from cod and furs, he hoped for a supply of ashes and oil for the Bristol soap works. But Guy was unsuccessful, and the first lasting settlement in Newfoundland was one established in 1618 at Bristol Hope, Harbour Grace.

Though international war ceased during James I's reign there was still trouble for Bristol ships and goods from pirates, including Turkish, and from privateers when war broke out again with Spain, and then France, in the 1620s. Privateers could be 'Biscayners' from northern Spain, or Dunkirkers. There was thus some naval activity in the Bristol Channel, with a small squadron cruising between Bristol itself and southern Ireland, under the command of the 'Admirals on the coast of Ireland'.

By now, in 1619 and 1620, there had been two sailings from Bristol to build up the settlements in Virginia whose first colonisation from England, ahead of the Pilgrim Fathers' in New England, had started in 1607. The ships were the *Margaret* and the *Supply*, one carrying settlers from near Berkeley, the other intending colonists from further north in Gloucestershire, near Winchcombe. John Smith of Nibley, Lord Berkeley's steward, was himself financially interested in the venture and gives exhaustive details of the scheme. The two ships had to be equipped with all the necessities of pioneering life; these included food and clothing, tools, building materials, fruit plants and seeds.

Many items were bought in Bristol at the St James's Fair, annually held towards the end of July and always a highly important commercial and retailing event. The details which Smith gives are of the greatest value in showing how much various goods cost in Bristol at that time. Some items, particularly weapons and martial equipment in 1619 and textiles in 1620, were bought in London, while tools such as felling axes and hoes were made in the Forest of Dean.

Alderman John Whitson, a leading Bristol merchant in the Spanish trade, served as mayor and the city's Member of Parliament; he was mayor in 1603–4, when Bristol had yet another severe outbreak of plague. He died in 1629 from a fall from his horse, leaving no male heir. In 1627 Whitson had made a will which settled most of his estate on the City corporation, for the novel purpose of founding a girls' school. The girls were to be daughters of deceased or 'decayed' freemen or burgesses, they were to wear red dresses (hence the title Red Maids for the school) and were to be bound apprentices to the schoolmistress. Only twelve girls were at first in the school, which opened in 1634 in a house near the Gaunts' building which already housed Queen Elizabeth's Hospital. The numbers soon increased and the buildings were expanded.

Spanish sherry sack would certainly have been a wine with which John Whitson, as a merchant, would have been familiar. When, in 1634, three officers – a captain, a lieutenant, and an ensign of the Military Company of Norwich – came to Bristol on a long tour of England, they noticed many things, particularly the churches with their 'Laudian' furnishings, the organs in the same churches, the bowling green and the local military company's training ground in the Marsh. They remarked on the prosperous state of the trade companies and on the range of Bristol's commerce. As they were leaving for Wells they were treated to a 'cup of Bristol milk', the first known reference to what was to become a famous sherry.

Three years before the Norwich cavaliers made their stop in Bristol a ship had left the port in search of the North-West Passage which, if found and successfully navigated, could lead to the Pacific and hence to the Spice Islands and Cathay. This ship, of only seventy or eighty tons, was commanded by Captain Thomas James, a Bristol man of Welsh origin who had started as a barrister but later became a seaman and commanded a privateer. He was backed by the Merchant Venturers, had an interview with Charles I, and named his ship the *Henrietta Maria* in honour of the queen. He left Bristol in 1631, sailed through the Hudson Strait and deep into Hudson's Bay, where James Bay, at the larger bay's southern tip, bears his name. He was obliged to winter there, suffered much hardship, and gave the name of Brandon Hill to a hill where he set up the royal arms, portraits of royalty and the arms of Bristol. In 1632 he sailed back, arrived in Bristol and saw Charles I. As he had literary gifts he wrote a book on his northern experiences which was published in 1633. After a further spell of naval service – against pirates – he fell ill and died in 1635.

By now, however, Bristol traders were much troubled by monopolies in the import and sale of such goods as tobacco, starch and soap. These monopolies were granted to court favourites who had little knowledge of the details of business. This was but one of the irritants which led to an atmosphere of discontent before the Civil War.

Religious Dissent and Civil Strife

Other points of controversy concerned religion. Soon after 1600 some groups in Bristol had started to hold worship not in accordance with the Book of Common Prayer. Such gatherings were on the wrong side of the law and were held – to escape unfavourable notice from the city magistrates – in the castle, which was still a Gloucestershire island on the edge of Bristol. The first of these gatherings, forming the nucleus of what came to be known as the Castle Green Congregational Church, was probably held in 1613.

The early meetings were in the private homes of members in the congregation. They also had help from the Puritan vicar of St Philip's Church, and later from a clergyman who came over from Gwent. Among the most fervent of those who organised and enlivened 'separatist' congregations was Mrs Dorothy Hazard, the widow of a grocer named Anthony Kelly. On Kelly's death, she defied the law by keeping her shop open on Christmas Day (a favoured Puritan target) and other holy days. Later, in 1639, she married Matthew Hazard, the vicar of St Ewen's. In the following year she formed a small congregation which held services not of the Prayer Book, but wifely loyalty induced her to come to St Ewen's to hear Hazard's sermons.

In 1642 came the first military action of the Civil War. There were, among Bristol's citizens, convinced supporters of both sides. But what most Bristolians really wanted was neutrality, to avoid destruction in a siege or storm, and the chance to continue the business and trading life which was vital to the chief urban centre in the West. The city's fortunes varied considerably from 1642 to 1645. These three years were full of incident. Bristol had two sieges, with an intervening period of Royalist rule, and became a resort of Royalist sympathisers from elsewhere.

From August 1642 there were various moves suggesting Bristol's eventual allegiance to the Parliamentary cause, and in November some earthworks were raised round the city in case it had to be defended; only Parliamentary troops were then in the area. Early in December Colonel Essex was admitted on behalf of Parliament, and on 9 December he took over the city. From Parliament's point of view he proved a most unsatisfactory governor, and two months later he was replaced by the lawyer Colonel Nathaniel Fiennes, a son of Lord Saye and Sele, who was known as 'Old Subtlety' and in those early days of the Civil War was a leading counsellor on the

Oliver Cromwell (left) and Colonel Nathaniel Fiennes, who for a time held Bristol for the Parliamentarians during the Civil War.

Parliamentary side. Soon after Fiennes took over there was a plot to seize Bristol for the king. Its leaders, merchants named Robert Yeamans and George Boucher, had various associates, including a son of the Bishop of Bristol and William Colston who later became eminent on the Royalist, or High Tory, side in national politics. The plot was soon discovered, and Yeamans and Boucher were executed, to become martyrs for the Royalist cause.

Soon after the defeat of Parliament's army at Roundway Down near Devizes, in July 1643, many Parliamentary supporters fled into Bristol. The first of Bristol's Civil War sieges soon followed, with Fiennes as the defender and Prince Rupert in command of the assaulting force. The defences were partly by the waterside, in the Marsh, and, on the Somerset side of the city, in the formidable wall between the Marsh and a spot on the Avon near the Temple Church. Higher up, there were fortifications on Brandon Hill, on the hill which was later crowned by the Royal Fort, along the ridge of Kingsdown and then down hill to Stoke's Croft and so to the river Frome. It was a long perimeter, and hard for Colonel Fiennes to defend with the forces available to him.

Prince Rupert made his first headquarters in the college buildings at Westbury-on-Trym. This was on 23 July, but the Prince soon moved closer in, and the first assaults were made on 24 and 26 July. Attacks were made on the Stoke's Croft fortifications and on the Prior's Hill Fort (at the far end of Kingsdown), which was held by Colonel Robert Blake. He later won fame as the successful defender of Taunton and as the 'General at Sea' under the Commonwealth. Colonel Wentworth, aided by Colonel Washington, successfully attacked the forts on Prior's Hill and Brandon Hill, eventually occupied College Green and accepted Colonel Fiennes' surrender. The attack on the southern defences, by a Royalist army from the West of England, was a tactical failure, but the repulse did not affect the main result.

Bristol had two years of Royalist occupation. It was the largest city in England held by the king, and was a rallying point, and refuge, for many Royalists coming in from areas held by Parliament. The port, with a few ships of the Navy (most of which had gone over to Parliament) patrolling the Bristol Channel, was a base for shipping in supplies and troops from Ireland and from predominantly Royalist South Wales. A mint and a printing press were set up in what was the economic capital of Royalist England; the Royalists' political capital, however, continued to be Oxford.

Prince Rupert added to Bristol's defences, most notably in the building of the Royal Fort, under the supervision of the well-known Dutch military engineer Sir Bernard de Gomme, who was in the service of the Royalists. The Royal Fort was built both to resist an attack and to dominate the city, and it became the prince's headquarters. Royally held Bristol was troubled, but never harmed, by the widespread forays, from Gloucester, of Colonel Massey.

The Battle of Naseby marked a decisive turn for the worse in the Royalists' fortunes, and the Battle of Langport, later in July 1645, eclipsed their last field army in the West. Bath, a Royalist city, fell on 29 July, and Fairfax and Cromwell decided on a speedy assault on Bristol. Their headquarters, where they held a council of war, were at Wick Court near Stapleton. Expecting an attack, Prince Rupert drew in his outposts at Clifton, Westbury-on-Trym and Bedminster, concentrating his defence on the Royal Fort, the lines along Kingsdown, Brandon Hill, and the southern defences. His main problem was that he did not have enough forces to man the entire fortified perimeter. On 1 September he made a sally which was driven back. The fort on Portishead Point had by now been captured, so that ships of Parliament's navy could come closer to Bristol's harbour.

The main attack, masterminded by Fairfax, came on 10 September. On the southern side it was repulsed, with heavy casualties, and the Parliamentary army had some difficulty in entering Prior's Hill fort at the eastern end of Kingsdown; when they did take it they put the Royalist defenders to the sword. Prince Rupert now realised that he could not hold Bristol and asked Fairfax for terms. Later that day, after his surrender of the Royal Fort, he marched out across Durdham Down, well mounted and richly clad. He was accompanied by many Royalists, including gentry and ladies, who had taken refuge in Bristol. Charles I was angry at his nephew's surrender of a city which, he hoped, could have been held for much longer, and perhaps relieved. Though Rupert was cleared of treachery and cowardice, the rift remained, and the word 'Bristol' could never be mentioned between Charles I and his nephew.

Colonel Philip Skippon now became the Parliamentarian Governor of Bristol. The City Council was soon purged of Royalist supporters, and a new mayor, John Gunning, and two new Members of Parliament were chosen. Some of the city clergy also lost their livings. Bristol, with the revival of its overseas trade, could now settle down to the new regime.

A dramatic and tragic episode concerned the treatment of the Bishop of Bristol, Thomas Howell, a Welshman, Oxford graduate, eloquent preacher, and a chaplain to Charles I. Parliamentary soldiers attacked the Bishop's Palace and unroofed it so that the rooms lay open to the weather. Mrs Howell, who already had at least eight children, was expecting again and died after her experience. The bishop himself was injured by the soldiers and died in 1646. Some of the none too extensive estates of the bishopric were confiscated. But no harm came to the cathedral and, unlike the cathedral at Exeter (where a wall from floor to vault separated Independent and Presbyterian congregations), it was never subdivided.

When civil war broke out again in 1648 the fighting was largely confined to South Wales. Cromwell, who moved west to quell the uprising, was most anxious that Bristol, the most important city in the West of England, should be reinforced and securely held.

The Commonwealth period in Bristol had no spectacular episodes to match the two Civil War sieges. The city's trade revived, and sugar refineries marked the beginnings of Bristol's vital, eventually pre-eminent, West Indian trade. The emigration of indentured white 'servants' started soon after 1650; it was still hoped that a white labour force could be built up to man the plantations. Bristol's coal-fired productive industry was in its early stages. Venetian expertise helped to start the glass industry, which produced mainly bottle and window glass, in about 1651, and pottery, a forerunner of Bristol delftware, was first made around this time, supplementing the products of the Ham Green kiln in northern Somerset.

Congregations meeting to worship contrary to the Anglican Prayer Book were now free to proliferate, though some proved not to be permanent, and Methodism remained well in the future. But one addition to the local Nonconforming scene, eventually both of religious and social note, did start its activity in these Commonwealth years. These were the Quakers, later known as the Society of Friends. They were not, in those early days, as quietist as they eventually became, and pacifism was to be a later development. John Camm and John Audland, in 1654, were the preachers who started the Bristol Quaker congregation. Tradesmen were among its members, and after meetings in an upper room in Broadmead they bought a plot in the site of the Dominican Friary and there in 1670 put up their first meeting house – hence the term Quakers' Friars.

In 1656, London and Bristol were the locations for spectacular events concerning James Naylor, a travelling Quaker preacher who attracted a large following. His devotees included some unstable characters who inspired Naylor with the heretical notion of his divinity. On the strength of this claim he rode into Bristol, with a few followers, in what amounted to a blasphemous parody of Palm Sunday. He was arrested, searched, and sent to London, where a committee of the House of Commons convicted him of blasphemy. He was pilloried, whipped through the streets, and had his tongue bored through with a red-hot iron. This punishment was repeated in

The heretic James Naylor and scenes depicting his torture.

Cromwell ordered its destruction, and the great tower keep built over five hundred years earlier by Robert of Gloucester was demolished. Only a few fragments remained within the area of some ten acres and the houses and shops of Castle Street arose on the cleared site.

After Cromwell's death in 1658, and in the last few months of the Commonwealth regime, there was a minor rising of apprentices, petitioning for a free Parliament, the repeal of some illegal duties, and the restoration of the monarchy. The revolt was easily put down, but it was clear that many Bristolians were ready for the political change which came in 1660.

The Restoration cleared the way for ecclesiastical and civil changes. Gilbert Ironside became Bishop of Bristol in 1661, a new dean was appointed to the cathedral, and the Horfield estate was handed back to the bishopric. Charles II and Queen Catherine visited Bristol in 1663, and the King knighted five leading citizens. Mayors, and members of the Corporation, were expected to be actively loyal to the restored monarchy, expressing their loyalty by practising Anglicanism according to the Prayer Book of 1662, and by making life as difficult as possible for Nonconformists. The Nonconformists themselves identified ten episodes of persecution between 1660 and 1688. But the main times of trouble were 1663–4; in 1674, when Bishop Carleton was notably active; in 1681, after Charles II's snap dissolution of the Parliament at Oxford, and in 1683 after the foiling of the Rye House plot.

In 1663–4, when the newly knighted and fervently Royalist Sir John Knight was mayor, some independent or Baptist members were put in prison; bad treatment and gaol fever caused the deaths of some. Their simple meeting houses were wrecked, and the pews, and what were mentioned as the 'prattling boxes' (pulpits) were burnt out in the street. Further attacks, urged on by Bishop Carleton, came in 1674, and caused the imprisonment, and death by illness in the Newgate Prison, of a Nonconformist minister.

Bristol. He later recanted his extreme claims, and for a time lived in Bristol as a practising Quaker.

Bristol lost one of its great landmarks in 1656. Perhaps fearing that the castle would become a refuge, not only for petty criminals but also for more active malcontents,

A leading chronicler of these harryings was Edward Terrill, a prosperous tradesman who became an elder of the Broadmead Baptist Chapel and was the compiler of the Broadmead Records. By his will of 1679 he provided for the foundation of the Baptist College for the tuition of young members of the local Baptist congregations who wished to enter the ministry. The work of the college, closely linked to the Broadmead Chapel, did not actually start till the 1720s.

The 1681 persecution involved the closure of all meeting houses, so that members of the congregations had to meet out of doors. The same happened in 1683, when some of those found attending a meeting on Brislington Common fled across the Avon. They were soon hounded back, some of them through the river, and one man, a linen draper, was drowned and a preacher nearly died.

These events did not impede the revival of Bristol's river and overseas trade. Tobacco from Virginia was particularly important, and during the Dutch war, in 1667, nine Bristol ships, and nine more from other ports, were burnt by Dutch raiders. In 1670 half of Bristol's ships trading overseas were said to be in the tobacco trade. Shipbuilding was mostly concerned with the production of merchantmen, but in the 1650s, and again under Charles II, Bristol was the scene of naval shipbuilding, the ships being much larger than those constructed for trading use. Some ships had their hulls built at Lydney, of oak from the Forest of Dean, and were then towed to Bristol for fitting out. Four warships, one of them a two-decker named the *Edgar*, were built at Bristol in Charles II's reign. The chief local shipbuilder, technically competent but apparently a difficult and foul-mouthed man, was Francis Bailey; some men were unwilling to work for him.

Charles II's reign was also the time for perspective views of Bristol, distinct from maps of the modern, two-dimensional kind. One came out in 1671, the other in 1673. Both were made by James Millerd, a mercer in Bristol who was active as a surveyor. That of 1671 is entirely a perspective, or bird's-eye view, of the city as seen from the south. The 'exact delineation' of 1673 is more like a map, with streets two-dimensionally shown, but also with churches, gateways, and gabled houses indicated in three dimensions. It is clear that the city had not yet expanded dramatically, and the suburbs were still fairly small. Houses are shown on the site of the castle, and also on that of the Royal Fort, which had been pulled down soon after the second siege. The arms of the city, the diocese, and of Charles II and Queen Catherine of Braganza (the arms of Portugal surrounded by the Garter) are displayed.

The river at high tide is shown with ships and seals in its water, while the marsh has a bowling green, dumped anchors and cannon, and pasturing sheep. Round the edge twenty little sketches give views of buildings in the city, a landscape rendering of the Bristol Channel from Cardiff to Aust, and one of Bath before its Georgian and Victorian expansion.

The demolished castle keep and the Royal Fort appear on the map, and of the buildings existing in 1673 Millerd shows: the cathedral; St Mary Redcliffe; the Customs House, then on Welsh Back; Bristol Bridge, now without its chapel but still lined with houses; the High Cross; one end of Christ Church; the Great House, and Canynges' mansion in Redcliffe Street.

The City Councillors were clearly pleased with Millerd's 'delineation', for they gave him a silver tankard worth £10.7s.8d, while the Merchant Venturers spent £5 on another tankard for him.

Two pleasant pen-pictures of Bristol survive from the reign of Charles II. One describes the visit, as part of a tour of western England to avoid the plague in London, of Marmaduke Rawdon, a London wine merchant. He found many equivalents in Bristol to institutions in London, among them the local trading companies, and the blue-coat boys, like those of Christ's Hospital, in the Queen Elizabeth's Hospital School. He notices the nails at the top

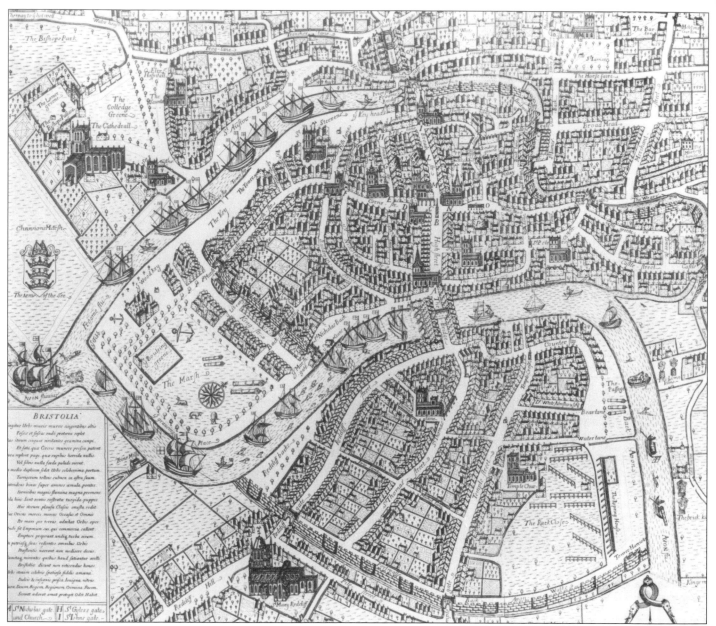

A detail from Millerd's perspective view of Bristol, 1673.

of Corn Street, describing them as 'brass pillars … for people to lean upon, to talk, tell money [hence the phrase "paying on the nail"] and to sign writings'. It was a time when more business was done outdoors than in the privacy of houses or offices. Rawdon comments on a scarcity of handsome women, noting further that Bristolians were 'not affable to strangers' and that sleds, rather than carts, were used to draw goods through the streets.

Samuel Pepys visited Bristol on 13 July 1668, while he was staying in Bath. He called on some local notables, and particularly the uncle of Deborah Willet, Mrs Pepys' serving maid who had been born in Bristol. He strolled through the streets and along the quay, which he calls a 'most large and noble place'. He also, as a high official in the Navy office, went to Bailey's shipyard, where he found that Bailey was out of town, but saw the hull of the *Edgar* which was then being built. A parting repast included a cold venison pasty, strawberries, table wine, and Bristol milk sherry. He saw the High Cross, which he compares to one at Cheapside in London.

Samuel Pepys, on a visit to Bristol in 1668, strolled along the quay and noted the sleds used for conveying wine and other goods.

One extension to Bristol's urban area had been finished in time for Millerd to notice it in 1673. This was King Street, named after Charles II, which impinged on the area of the Marsh and outside the line of the town wall between the Frome and the Avon arms of the harbour. On the north side a row of gabled houses had been put up about 1650, while at the eastern end St Nicholas's parish almshouses, gabled and with mullioned windows, had been built between 1652 and 1656. Another row of houses, to make it a 'street' worthy of its royal name, was now needed. This was built about 1664, leaving an open space, with a double row of trees and a view of the countryside, in the Marsh. The houses of this date were still timber-framed and gabled. One sees this most notably in the half-timbered range now occupied by the Landoger Trow inn; it once had five gables, but the two eastern ones were bombed in 1940.

Two years later, in 1666, the Great Fire of London consumed six-sevenths of the city. Timber-framed housing, of the type that had fared so badly in the fire, was soon prohibited in London. Bristolians took the hint, and no more houses of this type were put up to keep company with the numerous half-timbered houses, often with elaborate stone fireplaces, which survived in some streets till nearly the end of the Georgian era.

By this time some of the more prosperous and influential citizens had begun to move out to newly built mansions on the edge of the countryside. Sir Robert Yeamans had a house at Redland, and Sir Robert Cann, who already owned some farm property at Stoke Bishop, built himself the large and opulent mansion of Stoke House, with curved gables in the Dutch manner and a baroque porch with twisted columns, bearing the date 1669. Later in the seventeenth century the Jacobean mansion at Kingsweston was bought by the Southwells, to become the nucleus of what is now the famous Blaise Estate. The Hotwells Spa was another development on the edge of Bristol, and within the parish of Clifton, which, like Stoke Bishop, was still a part of Gloucestershire. The water of the spa gushed up through the tidal mud of the Avon at the top end of the gorge. In 1676 the Merchant Venturers acquired the relevant part of the manor of Clifton; they later bought the rest of the manor, including the right to exploit mineral rights and mineral water. The great days of the Hotwells Spa came, however, in the eighteenth century.

The succession to the throne became a dominant topic, in Bristol and elsewhere, in the last years of Charles II's reign. The king had no legitimate sons and there was nothing to prevent the accession of his brother James, the Duke of York, who had two daughters who could succeed him. What complicated the issue was James's announcement that he had become a Catholic. The accession of a Catholic was not illegal as the law then stood, but in a country now overwhelmingly Protestant, and with the ruling sovereign the head of the Established Church, it was most inadvisable. The last years of Charles II's reign were overshadowed by the Exclusion controversy, with the religious and political adversaries of the Duke of York attempting, as best they could, to ensure that James would not become king. But the Exclusion Bill never became law, and after Charles II's death early in 1685 the stage was set for armed risings to supplant him, if need be by one of his bastard sons. This, in the West of England, took the form of the Monmouth Rebellion, the rebel candidate being the royal bastard James, Duke of Monmouth.

The campaign started with Monmouth's landing at Lyme Regis and ended with his defeat at Sedgemoor. He was soon captured, and was executed in London. Though Bristol contained, among its Nonconformists and others, many potential members of Monmouth's makeshift army, its direct involvement in the short campaign was very small. The first Duke of Beaufort did much to ensure that no Bristol recruits found their way to Monmouth's force. Monmouth himself, at a stage in his campaign which included the occupation of Pensford in the Chew valley,

sent scouts to look down, from Knowle or Totterdown, on the southern wall of Bristol which had successfully resisted attack in the two Civil War sieges. The sight of some regular troops and a large body of the militia drawn up outside the wall seems to have deterred Monmouth, who was an experienced and skilful soldier, from making a direct attack on Bristol. He switched his plans to an assault through Bristol's undefended eastern outskirts, but this never materialised.

In the 'Bloody' Assizes Lord Chief Justice Jeffreys came to Bristol with one of his team of five judges. No rebels were due to be tried in the city, but Jeffreys suggested that some prosperous Bristol citizens, including the mayor, Sir William Hayman, should be brought to court for the kidnapping of local children to work, under conditions of semi-slavery, as indentured servants in the plantation colonies. A few of the rebels condemned to death in Somerset were hanged, as a spectacle intended to discourage armed rebellion, on Redcliffe Hill – the nearest point in Somerset to the city – where many Bristolians could easily go to watch the deterring spectacle.

The joint rule of William III and Mary II lasted from 1689 till Mary's death late in 1694. William then continued as sole sovereign. The 1690s give us another pen-picture of Bristol: the account of a visit by the traveller Celia Fiennes, daughter of Nathaniel Fiennes, who had surrendered Bristol to the Royalists in 1643. Celia Fiennes, like her father, was a Nonconformist, and in politics a Whig. She came into Bristol through Kingswood, where she noticed miners coming down into the city with 'horseloads' of coal. She mentions the cathedral and the parish churches, the houses which were 'most of timber work' and the streets which were narrow and hence 'something darkish'. She refers to the two almshouses at the eastern, or Old Market, entrance to Bristol, also to Edward Colston's 'noble almshouse', recalling a gentleman's house, on St Michael's Hill, with lodgings both for men and women, a kitchen, and a chapel. This was one of the first of Colston's many benefactions, to his native city, London and else-

Portrait of Edward Colston by Jonathan Richardson the elder.

Colston's many benefactions to his native city – tainted, some critics say, by profits from the slave trade – included schools and these almshouses on St Michael's Hill.

where. He bought the land in 1691, and when it was finished Colston's almshouse had the Merchant Venturers as its governors. Celia Fiennes also mentions Bristol's seaborne commerce, including the export of coal, Bristol Bridge with its houses, the Market Place, the High Cross, the walks round the Marsh, and the Hotwells, whose water was 'as warm as new milk'.

Two separate events soon occurred concerning the fine Jacobean half-timbered house which had been built by Robert Aldworth near St Peter's church. For several years it was used as a sugar refinery, and in William III's reign it briefly served another industrial purpose. In 1695 a decision was made to improve the currency, and in 1696 this was done by establishing five provincial mints: at Bristol, Chester, York, Norwich, and Exeter. The work at Bristol was carried out in this building and silver coins were made there to a total value of £457,896, each with a little capital B in a space below William III's head.

St Peter's Hospital: Robert Aldworth's fine Jacobean house, which later served as a sugar refinery, mint and home for paupers, was destroyed by bombing in the Second World War.

In 1698, after the mint was closed, the mansion became the headquarters of the Corporation of the Poor. This combined poorhouse for the Bristol parishes came into being as a result of John Cary's 'Essay on the State of England in Relation to its Trade' which came out in 1695. Cary was a Bristol merchant, and his book was the first to be published in his own city. A wide-ranging work, it suggests the establishment of specially organised work-houses, to supersede the haphazard and often ineffective system which had existed for nearly a century. In some places, including Exeter, the poorhouse was purpose-built, but in Bristol the one-time Aldworth house, unsatisfactory in many ways, was fitted out as a combined office for the Corporation of the Poor and as a home for the paupers; it had later to be extended and improved. It was known as St Peter's Hospital.

At the very end of the century, in 1699, plans were made for the building, along four sides of the Marsh, of a spacious and ambitious residential square. Building work took place in the first few years of the coming century, in time for the square, divided between the parishes of St Nicholas and St Stephen, to be called Queen Square in honour of Queen Anne, who visited Bristol in 1702.

The Peak Period: *1700–1760*

The building of Queen Square, with its handsome, brick-faced houses, proceeded in Queen Anne's reign, while a street running down along its western side was called Prince Street, after her husband, Prince George of Denmark, who died in 1708. A new Customs House was built in the middle plot along the square's northern side, replacing the old one on the Back, and conveniently placed for both arms of the harbour. Queen Square soon became fashionable as a district in which many of the merchant élite had their homes. Its main disadvantage was in its low-lying site, surrounded on three sides by the tidal river, in whose waters an 'assemblage of nastiness' floated and, if the tide failed to carry it out to sea, came back again to offend the eyes and nostrils of those living here. Eventually these conditions encouraged a move uphill to Clifton, where the absence of odours could be combined with views over the countryside of northern Somerset.

Bristol enjoyed considerable prosperity about this time. It was probably in the early years of the eighteenth century that it overtook Norwich as the second most populous city in England; it is a pity that no reliable population figures, or census returns, such as we have since

Queen Square, laid out in the early 1700s on open space once used for bull-baiting, was an early example of town planning.

Rysbrack's statue of William III dressed as a Roman emperor is widely reckoned to be the finest equestrian statue in Britain.

1801, exist to provide statistical proof. This was also the time of more charitable gifts to his native city by Edward Colston, who made his money in London and lived at Mortlake in Surrey. In 1706 he bought the Great House and there he established Colston's School for fifty poor boys. The Merchant Venturers were appointed its governors. Its regime reflected the strictly Royalist and High Tory views of the donor, who was a devoted member of the Church of England, and rigidly opposed both to Nonconformity and Whig politics. Colston stipulated that no boys from Colston's School should be apprenticed to Nonconformists; this corresponds to his insistence that 'no taint of Whiggism' should be in the books provided for the Temple Colston Charity School which he had also built.

In the mainly Tory Parliament of 1710 to 1713 Colston sat as one of the Members for Bristol. He died, aged eighty-four and a bachelor, in 1721. His other benefactions included sums handed over to St Bartholomew's and Christ's Hospitals in London, to the cathedral and many parish churches in Bristol, and in other counties to the newly built churches of St George's at Tiverton and St Anne's in Manchester. He also left money to increase the income of many poor church livings.

During Queen Anne's reign an attempt was made to establish a theatre in Bristol. The building, on St Augustine's Back, near the site of the present-day Colston Hall, was soon suppressed thanks to the anti-theatrical, puritanical activities of the vicar of the Temple Church. After various other uses the building eventually, with Gothic windows inserted, became the Countess of Huntingdon's Chapel. It was not till well into the 1720s that a playhouse, unimpressive as a building but conveniently on the Clifton side of the city boundary and thus outside the scope of the Bristol magistrates, was built on the Clifton side of Jacob's Wells Road. In this position it could entertain the visitors to the Hotwells, including many 'fashionables' who were accustomed to theatre-going in London.

The outbreak of another war – in this case against France and Spain under the rule of Philip V – meant campaigning on land, culminating in the great battles of Blenheim, Ramillies, and Oudenarde, and action at sea which included a new spell of privateering. Privateers – as distinct from pirates, whose ravages were indiscriminate – were armed merchantmen who had official permission, from the Crown or the Lord High Admiral, to attack and plunder the merchantmen of enemy countries. Bristol merchants took readily to this form of gain. The most ambitious and carefully planned venture was that of the ships *Duke* and *Duchess*, under the overall command of Captain Woodes Rogers. They planned to sail into the Pacific and there, off the coast of Lower California, to intercept and plunder the richly laden galleon which plied every year from Manila in the Philippines to Acapulco in Mexico. From there the cargo would be taken overland through Mexico and then sent in another ship, on a transatlantic voyage, to Spain.

This great privateering venture was financed by a consortium of Bristol merchants. The ships left Bristol in 1708, called at a port in Brazil (which, as a Portuguese possession, was allied territory), rounded Cape Horn into the Pacific, and so were set for attacks on Spanish shipping and on ports in the Viceroyalty of Peru, which covered present-day Chile, Peru, Ecuador, and Colombia. They called, as other privateers had done, at Mas a Tierra ('closer inland') in the Juan Fernandez group of islands, and there took off the Scottish seaman Alexander Selkirk, whose experiences formed some of the material eventually used by Defoe in *Robinson Crusoe*. Selkirk, as a skilled and experienced seaman, became one of Rogers' officers. The privateers then captured several Spanish ships, captured the port of Guayaquil in what is now Ecuador, extracted a fairly high ransom, and departed for the Galapagos Islands.

The privateers then moved north, to Lower California. That year, 1709, two ships sailed out from Manila instead of the usual one. Rogers captured the smaller of the two, which was a rich prize, but was repulsed by the larger galleon. The privateers had intended to come home by Cape Horn. But they gathered that the Spanish South American squadron was on the alert. So they sailed across the Pacific, called at Guam for provisions, sailed through the Dutch East Indies, and eventually came back to Europe in 1711, via South Africa, in a Dutch convoy. The voyage, with harmony among the crews of the two ships – and remarkably few deaths in action or from disease – had turned out to be a circumnavigation of the world. The profits of the voyage, despite payments to the East India Company, who claimed that the privateers had invaded the seas where they held a monopoly of English trade, were about one hundred per cent on the original outlay. Rogers' later career, which included two spells as Governor of the Bahamas, was much concerned with the suppression of the scourge of piracy.

Other privateering ventures, less ambitious and far-ranging than that of Rogers and his 'setters out', sailed from eighteenth-century Bristol, but only in times of war against France or Spain.

Another maritime activity could best be pursued in times of peace. This was the slave trade. By now it was accepted, and unquestioned from any moral or ethical standpoint, that the plantation colonies could be run only with a Negro labour force, Africans being shipped across the South Atlantic, preferably with the minimum of loss by death, from West Africa to the Caribbean colonies or the Carolinas and Virginia.

The slaving ships, not as a rule the best of those in the plantation trade, would sail to the coast of what are now Nigeria, Ghana, and Angola. They would there make contact with the local chieftains, supplying them, in exchange for slaves, with barter goods which included brass ware, textiles, weapons for use in tribal wars, gin and other spirits. The ships would have to lie at anchor, perhaps for several weeks, while they stocked up with an acceptable cargo. In war time they could thus be an easy prey for enemy warships or privateers; slaving, for this

An unintended memorial to Bristol's part in the inhuman transatlantic slave trade: the 1720 gravestone of Scipio Africanus, a teenage slave brought to Britain as a servant at the Earl of Suffolk's house in Henbury.

reason, increased considerably in times of peace.

Bristol merchants were deeply involved in this dreadful traffic, but the city may never have counted as England's premier slaving port. London was also involved, and Liverpool in time became the leading port in the whole process, including slaving, of the plantation trade. Early in the eighteenth century Daniel Defoe, in his *Tour through England and Wales*, reckoned that Liverpool would 'soon outdo Bristol'. It duly became overwhelmingly predominant as a slaving port, and the last English slaver sent out, in 1807, was a Liverpool ship.

The best of the West Indiamen were the 'direct runners', smart and beautiful ships of a fair size, for the most part ship-rigged. They would take out to the colonists all the needs of a prosperous middle-class life, including furniture, food and drink (from cheese and cider to bottles of Hotwell water), stationery, clocks and books. Their cargoes even included mural monuments, by Bristol or Bath monumental masons, to embellish colonial churches. Trash knives and felt hats (many produced near Bristol), for the slaves to wear when bent over their work in the tropical sun, were also part of the outward cargoes. The ships would come back with rum, semi-refined muscovado sugar, and ivory from Africa which had been brought across by the slavers.

In the peacetime year of 1787–8 over seventy direct runners sailed from Bristol for the West Indies, more than twice the number of slavers sent out from elsewhere. The Bristol West India Association represented the interests of the merchants trading with the sugar islands; in wartime they were particularly concerned with the protection of convoys, escorting warships and mounting guns in the West Indiamen.

The eighteenth century was thus a peak period for Bristol as a mercantile, maritime, and industrial city. Trade with continental Europe continued, with wine shipped in from Spain and Portugal as well as from France. Softwood timber was also brought in from Baltic and Scandinavian countries, much of it in foreign-owned ships from such ports as Danzig, Memel, Gothenburg, and Stockholm. The trade, which included bar iron for the making of railings, was notably brisk at the times of peacetime architectural expansion.

Bristol was also, thanks to the opening of the Avon navigation in 1728, the port of Georgian Bath. Stone could thus come down the Avon for use in Bristol itself and elsewhere. Up-river the barges could take softwood timber for use in the roofs and floors of Bath's houses, glass for its windows and slate for its roofs, paving stones from Winterbourne, for the pavements in front of terraces and parades, and bar iron from Sweden or Russia for the railings round the sunken areas in front of many of the houses. One may fairly say that the navigation of the Avon

was one of the keys to the completion of Georgian Bath. Consumer goods and luxuries for Bath and Bristol could come direct from the London area by the regular, if leisurely, service of freight wagons, or they could, like Rysbrack's statue of William III in 1736, be sent round from the port of London by sea. Bath stone could be freighted round in the reverse direction, but London's grime restricted its use in the capital.

The prosperous eighteenth century was also the time for Bristol's own architectural expansion. The Exchange in Corn Street, by the elder John Wood of Bath, is in the Palladian style and its front block is one of the best public buildings in England of the Georgian period; it was finished in 1743. Some good Georgian buildings, including the Coopers' Hall, were inserted into the somewhat earlier King Street. Alterations were made to some of central Bristol's churches, and one also had examples of 'area' expansion, starting with the eastward residential district which was begun, early in the century, with St James's Square and went on to include Brunswick and

The interior of The Exchange in Corn Street, designed by John Wood, was originally open to the elements.

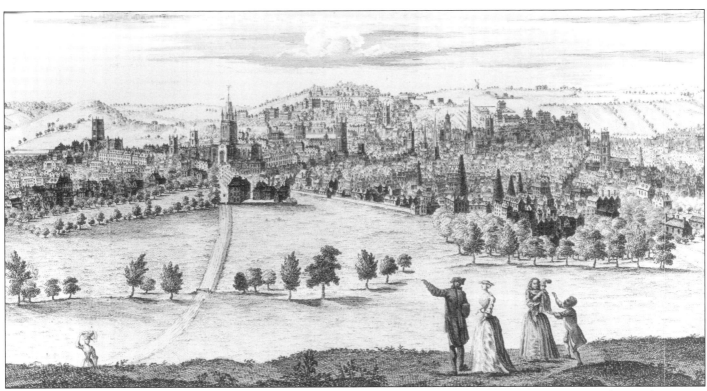

Buck's 'South-East Prospect of Bristol', 1734. The conical glass-making kilns for which Bristol was noted are prominent in the Temple area.

Portland Squares. Of greater social significance was the building of houses in College Green, Unity Street, and Orchard Street, and in the lower part of Park Street, which beckoned people uphill towards Clifton. Luxurious individual mansions, rather than the denser development of terraces and squares which would follow later, were built, in Clifton itself, by rich merchants who sought good air, fine views, and an unpolluted atmosphere.

Bristol now claimed to be the second largest city in England. This was certainly true about 1750, before the rise of Liverpool and some Midland and northern industrial towns. Seaborne commerce, however prosperous, could not by itself account for this proud status. The main cause was the combination, in the city itself and in its eastern outskirts, of coal-fired industry. This came in addition to shipping and the distribution of seaborne imports. It was vital for Bristol that, alone among southern England's cities, it had coalfields, both on its eastern side and eventually in southern Bristol.

The brass-founding trade, using copper ore shipped up from Cornwall and calamine from Somerset, was started in 1702 by Abraham Darby at Baptist Mills, where he could use the water of the Frome. As he needed more copious water than the Frome could provide, he soon started brassworks upstream on the Avon at Keynsham, where he used the water both of the Avon and its fair-sized tributary, the Chew. But in 1709 he left the Bristol area for Coalbrookdale in Shropshire, while the Bristol brass founders concentrated their activities in various up-river sites, with a sequence of brass mills along the course of the Avon.

Glass was another Bristol industry which used local coal for its furnaces. Production centred on window and bottle glass, but much clear 'flint' or lead glass, for drinking glasses and decanters, was also made. Many of the glasshouses were close to the Avon and in the southern area of the city. The conical tops of the furnaces, rising high above the working area, became as conspicuous in the local landscape as the steeples of the churches, and 'glass cones' are prominent in the views of Bristol produced in the 1730s by the prolific topographical recorders Samuel and Nathaniel Buck.

Local coal was needed for the firing of pottery kilns, as pottery, with the production of Bristol delftware and other

Late-eighteenth-century view from Clifton with a 'glass cone' in the foreground.

ceramic goods, was now another of Bristol's industries. The original pottery seems to have been made in St Anne's valley at Brislington. But later potteries were in the Redcliffe and Temple areas, not far from the glass kilns. All this was in the first half of the eighteenth century; the short period when porcelain was made in Bristol came well after 1750.

Shipbuilding was another trade which flourished in early Georgian Bristol. Merchantmen continued to be built locally, but some ships were 'plantation built' for Bristol merchants, tropical hardwoods being available to supplement the stocks of home-grown oak. There were still the problems arising from the muddy nature, at low tide, of Bristol's river harbour and its approach through the Avon Gorge. To lessen these hazards ships had to be sturdily built, giving rise to the phrase 'shipshape and Bristol fashion'.

Important events occurred, in eighteenth-century Bristol, outside the strictly economic field. The bishopric of Bristol continued to be one of the poorest in England and this, like the deanery, was always held in conjunction with some other, far better-paid post. Joseph Butler, who held the Bristol bishopric from 1738 till 1750, when he was moved to the much richer see of Durham, claimed that all his improvements in the Bishop's Palace at Bristol were paid for out of the income of the deanery of St Paul's, which he also held. Thomas Secker, who was Bristol's bishop from 1735 to 1737, was the only Bishop of Bristol to become Archbishop of Canterbury. At this time, some parish churches acquired new baroque or neo-classical fittings and furnishings. These included altarpieces and a splendid organ case at St Mary Redcliffe (then still known as Ratcliffe Chappel).

Bishop Butler said, of some of the more emotional displays of religious feeling, that 'enthusiasm is a very horrid thing'. Enthusiasm, of a type that the bishop disliked, was amply displayed by some of the converts of John Wesley. Bristol and its outskirts were the scene of much preaching by both George Whitefield and John Wesley; a great deal turned on how far their preaching could be done out of doors rather than in the churches.

Whitefield, though born in Gloucester, had Bristol connections on his mother's side. He had crossed the Atlantic to colonial Georgia, where his preachings were called 'enthusiastical whimsies'. He came back to Bristol, and though he was an ordained minister of the Church of England he, like John Wesley when he came to the district, was denied the use of Anglican pulpits. Instead, he held open-air preaching sessions in Bristol's eastern outskirts. This was in February 1739. Encouraged by his success, he also preached out of doors to the coal miners, who worked in their shallow pits and mostly lived in scattered cottages in the Kingswood area.

Later in the same year John Wesley was persuaded to preach at Hanham Mount. But he basically preferred the indoor facilities of a church, so in the later months of 1739 he started the building of the 'New Room' in Broadmead. An inscribed stone, laid by John Wesley, remains on one side of the chapel. Enlarged in 1748, the chapel was a suitable place for the decorous instruction of converts and the members of the 'religious societies' of the type encouraged by Bishop Butler. It was in the parish of St James, and John Wesley often took his hearers to communion services there. But out in Kingswood, among the miners, Wesley's preaching gave rise to spectacular displays of the convulsions and weepings which accompanied conversions, and the turning back of the converts from rough and brutal ways. The children of the miners also attracted John Wesley's attention and a school was opened for them in 1748.

Bristol thus became one of the most important centres of early Methodism, still a fervent, emotional subsection of the Anglican Church. Above the New Room were overnight sleeping quarters for Wesley's preachers who passed through Bristol. John Wesley was only occasionally in the city, but his brother Charles lived in Bristol for over

This 1918 painting by W.H.Y. Titcomb depicts John Wesley preaching in St Mark's before the Mayor and Corporation of Bristol in 1788.

twenty years, guiding and supervising the local Methodists and writing many of his well-known hymns.

Theological differences eventually caused a rift between John Wesley and George Whitefield, who inclined to Calvinism. Whitefield built his own tabernacles in Kingswood and in Penn Street in central Bristol in 1753. This latter originally counted as a chapel within the Church of England, and the Countess of Huntingdon attended the opening of a building in which the services were 'decorous and ecclesiastical'. The chapel later became a Congregational place of worship.

Edward Terrill's Baptist College got a new principal in 1720, and its continuous work really started from that time, over forty years after Terrill's will inaugurated the project. The college remained closely linked to the fortunes of the Broadmead Chapel.

Benevolent activity extended to the organised care of the sick. The eighteenth century saw the founding of

The statue of Wesley outside the New Room in Broadmead was set up in 1933 to mark the 200,000 miles he covered on horseback to preach throughout England.

county infirmaries, to receive poor invalids. One of the earliest of these infirmaries was later known as the Bristol Royal Infirmary. The project was launched, and the first subscriptions came in, during 1736. Some houses already standing in Marlborough Street were adapted, and the first patients were admitted in 1737. Dr John Bonython, who came from Cornwall and had been at Cambridge, was one of the pioneers and the first of the Infirmary's physicians. John Elbridge, the Collector of Customs, who came from colonial America, was a leading benefactor, and his legacy made it possible to extend the buildings. From 1749 the motto 'Charity Universal' was used for the Infirmary. Many of its early supporters were Quakers, and a Tory political bias was apparent among many of the staff.

Because of its prominence as a commercial and trading city, Bristol inevitably emerged as a major banking centre, too. Bankers, in those days, were closely allied to gold-smiths. A bookseller who ran a small banking concern was the son of a goldsmith, and John Vaughan, who was the City Corporation's banker till 1750, was also a goldsmith by trade. In 1750 Bristol's first banking partnership was formed; long afterwards it was known as 'The Old Bank'. Others soon followed, with various men of business among their directors. By the end of the eighteenth century there were seven banking concerns, all with their offices in the old centre of the city. Bristol's economic life had come far, and the city had yet to be surpassed by other commercial and industrial centres.

The Later Georgian Scene

George III's reign, which started in 1760, lasted sixty years, the last nine of which were those of the 'Regency'. Important commercial and economic events now occurred, but the period also saw the beginning of Bristol's decline when compared to other centres of shipping and manufacturing. The second half of the eighteenth century also included events of note in the literary story both of Bristol and in that of England as a whole. Other cultural episodes included the rise of the drama, and the building of the theatre, in King Street, which in 1778 obtained its royal licence and the right to be called the Theatre Royal.

King Street, with the Coopers' Hall and the Theatre Royal, in the early nineteenth century.

Bristol was still deeply concerned with transatlantic trade, with goods coming in from North America and the plantation colonies, notably from the sugar-producing islands in the West Indies. Jamaica, the largest of the West Indian islands under British rule, was now the most important and productive. Its newspapers were taken in Bristol, and its plantations had names which recalled localities in the Bristol area, such as Stapleton and Clifton. In one Jamaican newspaper there was an advertisement for the return of a runaway slave named 'Bristol'.

Bristol's overseas trade had links with the city's representation in Parliament and some of its Members of Parliament came from local merchant families. An exception was Robert Nugent, who started as a Member for a pocket borough in Cornwall and was a friend and money-lender to Frederick, Prince of Wales, the father of George III. He later became Viscount Clare in the Irish peerage and as an Irish peer could sit in the House of Commons. From 1754 he was Member for Bristol, but his hostility to colonial interests put him out of sympathy with his constituents. In their search for a new, more congenial Member the Bristol merchants and traders turned to Henry Cruger and Edmund Burke.

Georgian Bristol was not a 'pocket borough', in which a mere handful of voters had to be persuaded or 'treated'. It had over five thousand voters, and candidates often found that financial embarrassment, or even bankruptcy, went with success in a Bristol election. Henry Cruger was born in colonial New York in 1739 and was of Dutch extraction. He studied at King's College (now Columbia University), then came to Bristol to work in the office of

A page from the town clerk Robert Ricart's Calendar of 1479 showing the swearing-in of the mayor in Bristol's Guildhall.

Maritime Bristol in the nineteenth century.

A detail from the Merchant Venturers' almshouses in King Street.

Colston's almshouses on St Michael's Hill.

William Halfpenny's Coopers' Hall in King Street, now part of the Theatre Royal.

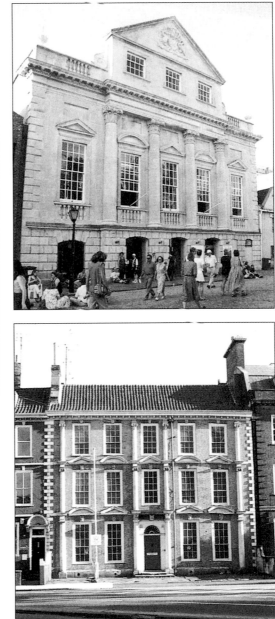

John Wood the elder's Palladian-fronted Exchange in Corn Street, 1743.

Houses in eighteenth-century Queen Square.

St George's church, from Great George Street, now used as a concert hall.

Cabot Tower on Brandon Hill.

Interior of the Elizabethan Red Lodge on Park Row, built in 1590 as a lodge to John Yonge's Great House, which stood on the site of the present Colston Hall.

Another magnificent interior: the Georgian House, 7 Great George Street, was once the home of John Pinney, a West Indies merchant. William Wordsworth stayed with the Pinney family in the 1790s and is said to have first met Coleridge there.

Part of the splendid glass collection on display in the Harveys Wine Museum, Denmark Street.

Entrance to the original Temple Meads railway terminus.

The elegant Clifton Suspension Bridge over the Avon Gorge.

Castle Park, with sculpture by Peter Randall-Page and the ruins of St Peter's church in the background.

Welsh Back, looking towards Bristol Bridge.

St Augustine's Reach during the Festival of the Sea, 1996.

Cruger and Mallard, the family firm. He married the daughter of a Bristol merchant and was a member of the City Corporation and a churchwarden of St Augustine's the Less, near the cathedral. He was readily chosen in 1774 as one of the City's Whig Members of Parliament. His colleague, sponsored and encouraged by the Quakers Joseph Harford and by Richard Champion, now the owner of Bristol's porcelain factory, was Edmund Burke. Cruger, with his strong local connections, topped the poll. Burke came next, not far ahead of the local merchant, Matthew Brickdale.

Edmund Burke was one of Bristol's representatives in Parliament for six years, from 1774 to 1780. He was, in some ways, an unsatisfactory Member for this particular constituency. He soon disagreed on important points with his colleague Henry Cruger, and when elected he declared himself free to vote on the merits of each case as it came up, and not as a Member for Bristol, which had its own special trading and economic interests, and where the views of the local merchants were often at variance with the supporters of other causes. Only twice, in 1775 and 1776, did Burke come in person to Bristol, and for the last few years of that session, when opposition to the king's policy on colonial America was seen to be of no avail, Burke and other Rockingham Whigs virtually withdrew from Parliament. A policy of conciliation with the American colonists, which Burke actively supported, alienated him from his Bristol constituents.

When hostilities broke out in 1775, the West Indian and North American trade was drastically affected, both by the interruption of sailings to and from the colonies, and by the ravages of colonial American privateers. The situation worsened in 1778 when France formally declared war. In 1782 Rochambeau's army played an important part in the defeat of Cornwallis's army and the surrender at Yorktown, which 'turned the world upside down'. By then the election of 1780, which he declined to contest, had ended Burke's Parliamentary link with Bristol. He knew that his position was hopeless, and that it was made worse by his support of greater economic independence; this alienated him from many Bristol merchants.

Cruger was defeated in 1780, but maintained his links with Bristol. He was mayor in 1781, and Bristol's Member of Parliament in 1784. In the end he went back to America, became a senator in the State of New York, and died as late as 1827.

Bristol's transatlantic trade soon revived after the Peace of Paris ended the war in 1783; it included a resumption of slaving, and the stocking up of the slave-labour force in the plantation colonies. The economic revival lasted for ten years, till in 1793 the outbreak of the French Revolutionary (later the Napoleonic) War caused serious financial restrictions on trade in Bristol, Bath, and other developing towns.

Once the American colonies became fully independent, and even after the occupation of Boston in 1776, many colonists who were not content to continue living in the United States found their way to England, a fair number of them to Bristol. Some had suffered, physically

Edmund Burke. His support for greater economic independence for the American colonies made him an unpopular Bristol MP.

or otherwise, before they left America, and unless they also had property in the West Indies they were compelled to live modestly. Most were from Massachusetts, though some came from New York, which held out for the Crown till 1783, and from other colonies. In Bristol they formed their own social circle. A large proportion lived in or near College Green, and James Boutineau, a Bostonian of Huguenot extraction who died in 1778, had a mural monument in St Augustine's the Less. Some of these Boston loyalists had served as lieutenant-governors of Massachusetts and one, Thomas Hutchinson, as a full governor.

Eighteenth-century Bristol had a wide range of weekly newspapers, but no daily paper appeared before the *Western Daily Press* in the 1850s. A news and advertisement sheet called the *Bristol Post Boy* came out in 1702 but did not last long. Two other productions appeared in 1713, published by a Quaker, Samuel Farley, whose family long dominated the local journalistic scene, the best known of their publications being *Felix Farley's Bristol Journal*. The *Oracle* papers came out in the 1740s, and *Bonner and Middleton's Bristol Journal*, started by Samuel Bonner, who had been a clerk with the Farleys, was launched as a rival to the Farley papers. There was more coverage, by means of newsletters coming down from London, of foreign and international news than there was of local events, though the news of the arrivals of ships and of visitors to the Hotwells and Bath are of much historical value; so too are advertisements of local and West Indian interest.

Bristol continued to grow in the latter half of the century. Eastward expansion included the building of Brunswick Square and Portland Square. The name of the latter honoured the Duke of Portland, who was twice Prime Minister and in 1786 was made Lord High Steward of Bristol. The ancient centre of the city saw rebuilding, such as that of Christ Church between 1787 and 1790, rather than completely new structures. Bristol Bridge was, however, replaced by the present three-arched one in the 1760s. The widening of High Street to give better access to the new bridge meant pulling down St Nicholas's church, whose sanctuary lay over the old St Nicholas's Gate. The new church, above a surviving medieval crypt, was in a neo-Perpendicular style, perhaps recalling that of the older building. It was, however, the time for a splendid plaster ceiling in the rococo taste, the work of Thomas Stocking the local plasterworker; this ceiling was a sad casualty of the bombing in 1940. The architect, both for the bridge and St Nicholas's, was James Bridges, who had worked in Pennsylvania and retired to the West Indies.

The 1760s saw a fair amount of Bristol building work in the ogee-headed Gothic style, much more than in Bath at the same time. It appeared in some houses, in Blaise 'Castle' by Robert Mylne at Henbury, in old St Michael's Rectory, and on the façade of Arno's Court, on the way to Brislington. This latter building, the residential element of a larger group, had a tunnel under the road leading to the bathhouse, with its rococo plasterwork and a fanciful Gothic colonnade, and also to the castellated stable block. The black slag blocks (from the local copper works) and whitish stone dressings of the stable block created a striking effect which led Horace Walpole to call Arno's Court 'the Devil's Cathedral'.

Started in 1740, King Square, a charming enclosure with different styles on its four sides, took its name from George II but was finished after his reign. Above King Square the steep slope of Kingsdown was intersected, along the contour and uphill. Dove Street was of humble dwellings, but Somerset Street was more impressive; the street fronts of its houses were unambitious, but the back elevations were imposingly treated, often with bow-windowed storeys one above the other, to command fine views over eastward-expanding Bristol and its immediate and more distant countryside. Kingsdown Parade, closer to the top of the ridge, followed later, with Georgian houses but a less exciting prospect.

Another area of growth was College Green and uphill in the direction of better air, and eventually to Clifton.

Interior of the new Christ Church, designed by William Paty, whose family produced a wealth of ornament in eighteenth-century Bristol buildings.

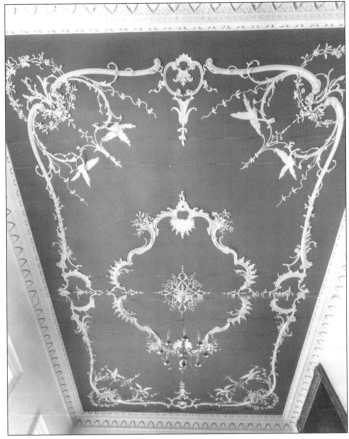

Rococo plasterwork on a ceiling in the Royal Fort.

Unity Street, on the east side of College Green, saw the construction of well-composed and stone-faced houses. Lower down, on the western side, College Street consisted, till it was pulled down in the 1950s for a municipal car-park, of modest houses with pleasing bow windows, also seen in Cumberland Street off Brunswick Square. The upward growth started with the lowest stretch of Park Street, soon a fashionable street in which to

live and at first purely residential; only one original doorway has survived the inroads of the plate-glass shop fronts which now give the street its commercial character. The first phase reached the bottom of Great George Street, whose lowermost houses are mid-Georgian in character and include two 'Gibbsian' doorways with flanking voussoir blocks. Higher up, Great George Street is distinctive with its large, individual houses for prosperous merchant families. Higher still Charlotte Street, started in 1787 and named after George III's queen, is a steeply rising terrace now with some balconies. The topmost element in this development is Berkeley Square.

The designers of much of this work, and the leading architects in Georgian Bristol, were the members of the Paty or Patty family, some of whom were also talented carvers, and produced both ornamental stonework and church monuments. The most prominent were James Paty,

This corner house in Dowry Square housed Dr Beddoes' Pneumatic Institution, where Humphry Davy experimented with 'laughing gas'.

Eighteenth-century arts and crafts in Bristol: (top) baroque ironwork gates by William Edney in St Stephen's church; (centre left) Bristol porcelain teapot made in Richard Champion's factory, c. 1775; (centre right) tin-glaze earthenware bowl and (bottom) glass by Lazarus and Isaac Jacobs in the city's museum and art gallery.

Clifton in the early 1800s.

his son James, Thomas Paty, who had a long and prolific career, and William Paty, who designed the new Christ Church and some of the mansions in Great George Street. Among his schemes started late in the 1780s was the range at the eastern end of Royal York Crescent, a project finished, along with much else in upper Clifton, only after the Napoleonic Wars.

The heyday of the Bristol Hotwells was in the eighteenth century, when many fashionable visitors came there, mainly in the months between April and October. It was thus a summer spa, with nearby Bath a mainly winter resort. Some of the Hotwells habitues moved to Bath when the Hotwells season was over; a similar move was made by the tradesmen who flourished on spa custom.

The Hotwell water, gushing up through the tidal mud at a moderate temperature, was recommended, somewhat doubtfully, for young ladies with consumption. Architectural expansion at the Hotwells was on a modest scale. It included the charming colonnade curving round to the Pump Room, and had some brick-faced houses, in Dowry Parade and Dowry Square, typical of what Bristol builders were then putting up.

The Hotwells Pump Room was of fair size, but no rival to the style and dignity of the Pump Room and Assembly Rooms at Bath. In the same riverside parish of Clifton individual mansions, along the road to the Downs, were accompanied by terraces and formal compositions like those at the top end of the Mall. Jane Austen was a visitor, for a short time, to upper Clifton. But as her sister Cassandra was there at the same time, Jane's letters contain no pen-pictures of this resort.

Bristol's literary associations in the eighteenth century mainly concern Chatterton, Hannah More, and the pioneer Romantics. There were also some minor poets, including Ann Yearsley the milkwoman who, in those days before pasteurised and hygienic dairying, kept her cows on Clifton Down and wrote under the alias of 'Lactilla', fell foul of Hannah More, a would-be benefactor, and died, perhaps insane, at Melksham in Wiltshire.

Thomas Chatterton was born in 1752, the posthumous son of the master of the charity school in Redcliffe parish; his father was also a singing clerk in Bristol Cathedral. St Mary Redcliffe Church and the younger William Canynges were important influences on his life and the subject of many of his mock-medieval poems. For seven years from 1760, he was at Colston's School in the Elizabethan 'Great House'. He was then apprenticed to John Lambert, a local attorney, and produced much of his poetry during those years. Lambert dismissed him when he found a paper with proposals for suicide. In 1770, Chatterton made his way to what he hoped was the more promising literary scene of London. There, after a hopeful start, he committed suicide.

Many of Chatterton's poems purport to be the work of Thomas Rowley, a priest whom the poet makes the secretary and close confidant of William Canynges; the

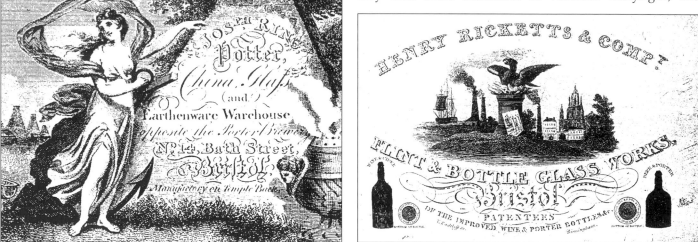

Early nineteenth century trade cards advertising Bristol china, glass and earthenware.

Imaginary scene from the childhood of the precocious poet Thomas Chatterton painted by Henrietta Ward in 1873.

surname Rowley is that of a Bristol merchant commemorated by a brass in St John the Baptist's church. The language of these 'Rowley' poems is medieval, of a type that some critics questioned even at that time of the early development of scholarly medieval studies. Chatterton's Bristol associates included Catcott, who was both a pewter maker and a would-be antiquarian, Burgum who was Catcott's partner in pewtering, and William Barrett, who combined work as a male midwife and local historian. None of them could be of real help to a youth who certainly had a poetic gift and whose poems, in the English of his own time, or rendered into it from the 'Rowleian' original, had genuine merit and anticipated some work of the Romantic Revivalists.

At weekends Chatterton was glad to wander in the highly 'romantic' scenery of the Avon Gorge, and knew the Jacob's Well Theatre before the opening of the Theatre Royal. He also knew, and appreciated, the interior of St Mary Redcliffe church; this was at a time when sympathy for Gothic was one of the roots of the Romantic Revival. He also sent some of his verses to Horace Walpole, who liked them at first, but cooled off when he learned of the ungenteel circumstances of the writer's life. Chatterton's mother and sister (Mrs Newton) outlived the poet and died in 1803 and 1807 respectively, having lent Chatterton's London letters to the clergyman – and eventually baronet – Herbert Croft, who returned them after a cruelly long time, but not before publishing the best account of Chatterton's short period in London.

Hannah More was born in 1745, one of five daughters of Jacob More, the parish school master of Stapleton parish, the school being at Fishponds, over a mile from Stapleton Village and on the other side of the Frome. She had advantages which Chatterton lacked, for her father lived till she was thirty-eight and had local influence. She was also a sincere churchwoman, and devoted the last part of her long life to social and religious work, with bishops and philanthropists among her many correspondents. She and her sisters moved into Bristol and there

St Mary Redcliffe church: this 1828 drawing by T.L.S. Rowbotham shows the church, before its spire was reinstated, and the nearby streets much as Chatterton would have known them.

opened a well-patronised boarding school for young ladies near the bottom of Park Street. Rich and influential people were among her patrons and she soon took up a literary career, with the writing of plays among her activities. She became friendly with David Garrick, and her play *Percy* of 1777 was a financial success although of no literary merit. She was the companion of Garrick's widow, who lived near London, in the last years of her life.

St Mary Redcliffe seen from the river (Rowbotham, 1826).

She eventually left Bristol to live at Cowslip Green and then in the substantial cottage of Barley Wood in Wrington. She there did charitable and missionary work among the rough calamine miners in the Mendips. Her literary output swung round to religious tracts and resulted in the 'improving' novel *Coelebs in Search of a Wife*.

Hannah More (left), the Bristol 'blue-stocking', and her protégée Anne Yearsley, whose life was described as 'a dignified struggle with honest poverty'.

Samuel Taylor Coleridge, who first met William Wordsworth in Bristol. The Bristol publisher Joseph Cottle published their Lyrical Ballads *in 1798.*

Her sisters all died before her, and after serious trouble with cheating servants she moved back into Bristol, and died at Clifton in 1833.

In the late eighteenth century Bristol was briefly a haunt of some of the famous poets of the Romantic Revival. Southey was born in Bristol in 1774 and spent much of his early life in the city. Coleridge came in 1794, and he and Southey lodged in College Street. Wordsworth also visited and they probably met in the Great George Street mansion of the Pinneys, who were West India merchants with estates in Nevis. Coleridge and Southey married the Fricker sisters, at St Mary Redcliffe, in 1795. This was at the time of their scheme, which they called Pantisocracy, under which they were to found an overseas colony, in which all members would have equal power, on the banks of the Susquehannah in Pennsylvania.

They belonged to the Bristol Library Society, founded in 1772, and the record of their borrowings is in the City Library, to whose original building, in King Street, the Society added a new wing. After his marriage Coleridge moved to Clevedon, but soon returned to Bristol, finding the walk into Bristol too long and tiring. Wordsworth at this time lived at Alfoxton in the Quantocks. He and Coleridge now made plans for the publication of a book of poems, and in 1798 the slim volume, *Lyrical Ballads*, was published in Bristol by the printer Joseph Cottle. Its best-known poem is Coleridge's 'Ancient Mariner', and it counts as one of the most innovative works of the Romantic Revival. Like many pioneering works it was not a financial success for its authors or its publisher.

The establishment of theatres was a risky venture at this time of residual Puritanism. The first efforts to set one up in Georgian Bath were frustrated, and the theatre on St Augustine's Back in Bristol, started in Queen Anne's reign, was soon shut and the building was turned over to other uses. A local clientele for such a venture was uncertain. So the first theatre, easy to reach by the theatre-going 'fashionables' who stayed at the Hotwells, was opened on the Clifton side of Jacob's Wells Road by the actor-cum-dramatist John Hippisley in 1729.

Later in the eighteenth century, some Bristol citizens, mostly merchants, raised a subscription to build a new, more central theatre. They chose a site off the northern side of King Street next to the Coopers' Hall, which had been built in the 1740s. The proprietors, as they were called, then sent some of their members to visit two theatres in London, and the new playhouse in Bristol was modelled on Drury Lane Theatre, which is said to have been designed by Sir Christopher Wren. Plans were obtained from the carpenter of Drury Lane, and Thomas Paty was the architect locally responsible. The foundation stone of the new playhouse in King Street was laid in 1764 and the building was opened on 30 May 1766. The first performance had to be billed as 'a concert of music and a specimen of rhetoric'. David Garrick wrote a prologue for the occasion, and though he never performed in the theatre he described it as 'the most complete, of its dimensions, in Europe'. A royal licence, avoiding the risk of prosecution, was obtained in 1778, and for some years the Theatre Royal at Bristol, which at first was open only in the summer (the Hotwells season), was served by the same company of actors as that in the Theatre Royal at Bath. It soon became one of the leading theatres outside London.

The City Library in King Street, patronised by both Coleridge and Wordsworth, is now a restaurant.

Ship movements were still much restricted by the tortuous approach through the Avon Gorge and the river harbour itself could be used only on a rising or full tide. Coasters and small craft could navigate the river on their own, but larger ships, including West Indiamen, had to be towed up the gorge by flotillas of rowing boats based on Pill. Some ships came no further than Pill or Hungroad, discharging their cargoes into small lighters which then came up the Avon to the quays. Shipbuilding was an active trade in Bristol in the eighteenth century, including some frigates built for the Navy in the 1770s and 1780s, and a two-decker, the *Nassau*, put afloat in 1785.

Other Bristol industries continued as before, with local coal mining a vital enabling factor. Brassware continued to be produced, and the copper works at Warmley, relying on coal from the local pits, at the top of the Lodge Hill, were one of England's largest industrial plants. In 1782 patent shot was first produced, in the shot tower close to St Mary Redcliffe, by William Watts, who also (disastrously) went in for speculative building at Windsor Terrace in Clifton.

Glass-making continued in the furnaces whose cones were conspicuous on the skyline of central Bristol, with moulded bottles eventually replacing blown glass. Ornamental Bristol glass, mostly blue, and with some pieces picked out with decoration in gold, was made by the Jewish firm of Isaac and Lazarus Jacobs, who came to England from Frankfurt. Soap-making was also carried on, though there were fewer firms in this trade than in the early years of the eighteenth century, and the manufacture of drinking chocolate also featured among Bristol's trades, albeit on a small scale compared to the later achievements of Fry's. Wine was copiously imported, and the origins of what became the firm of Harvey's date from the 1790s. Another wine merchant from that period, Averys of Bristol, was still flourishing two hundred years later.

Bristol's merchants were well aware of the severe disadvantages of their up-river and muddy harbour compared with Liverpool's open estuary. A wet dock had

The bustling nineteenth-century waterfront, now the site of the Bristol Centre.

been built, at the mouth of the River Trym at Sea Mills, in 1712. It was used by some privateers and also by whalers, but it was too far from central Bristol to be of real use, and the Seamills Dock Company lasted only till 1761. William Champion's 'Great Dock' was built in the 1760s, was soon taken over by the Merchant Venturers and became known as the Merchants' Dock. Several other projects were then put forward, all for 'dockising' the Avon from a point not far above the gorge. In 1791 William Milton, who was vicar of the Temple Church, put forward a scheme which allowed for a 'New River' to take the tidal flow of the Avon. This, in essence, was the same as the project for harbour improvement proposed, in 1802, by the London civil engineer William Jessop. This scheme had Parliamentary approval in 1803, and work started in 1804, involving drastic changes in the Bristol scene. The essence of the work now done was the 'New Cut', an artificial channel about two miles long, cut through earth and rock to take the natural flow of the Avon, with a main entrance basin (the Cumberland Basin) in Rownham Mead near the top end of the gorge.

The river harbour between those two points was to become the 'Floating' Harbour, in other words a harbour in which ships could float at all stages of the tide outside. As water would be lost each time the lock gates of the Cumberland Basin were opened to let ships in or out of

The Old Floating Dock, Hotwells, in the 1820s.

the Floating Harbour it would be topped up, or fed, by water from the new 'Feeder' Canal, a new and straight channel about a mile long, from Netham Weir, to the top end of the Floating Harbour. The New Cut and the Feeder were thus the chief additions to the geography and scene of the city. A second entrance to the Floating Harbour, from the New Cut through Bathurst Basin, where the millpond of Treen Mills was specially widened out, was also provided.

The New Cut, the Feeder Canal, and the Floating Harbour with its two entrance basins were finished in 1809, and a dinner was given by the Docks Committee to the paid labourers, English and Irish, but not to the French prisoners of war who had been put to work on its construction. The walls of the Cumberland Basin were not yet finished, so the first ships to enter the Floating Harbour came in through the Bathurst Basin. The cost of the undertaking had been nearly £600,000, about twice as much as Jessop's estimate, and the directors of the Bristol Dock Company had to charge dock dues so high that much trade was driven from Bristol to other ports such as Liverpool. The Floating Harbour was also finished too late to be of real use to the larger ships, particularly steamships, which were developed in the nineteenth century. The ultimate solution had to be the building of the dock at Avonmouth. In the meantime the New Cut, with its grassy banks, became a scenic feature in its own right, and a good carriage route, avoiding various inconveniences in the middle of the city, from Bath to the Hotwells or upper Clifton.

The living standards of Bristol's manual workers, particularly the unskilled labourers, were still pitifully low. Glasshouse workers, who toiled in almost intolerable heat and dirt, received more than other skilled craftsmen. But conditions were mitigated by locally available coal and by the numerous charities, including almshouses and charity schools, created in Bristol by centuries of organised philanthropy. Liverpool, though now larger than Bristol, had far fewer people in almshouses and charity

schools, and twice as many in workhouses. Almshouses continued to be increased by new benefactions. The Infirmary had now been enlarged by the erection of a new, and larger building between 1784 and 1792, with Thomas Paty as its architect; the building still exists, in a much altered state.

Bristol was also the scene of a pioneering asylum for the insane, started by a Quaker doctor and owing much to the example of 'The Retreat' at York, also started by a Quaker family, the Tukes. The founder was Dr Edward Long Fox, of the Falmouth family and a relative of Caroline Fox the diarist. He began work in a house at Downend and in 1804 started to construct the long building on the outskirts of Brislington, purpose-built for the accommodation of the insane. The less serious cases could be taken out for carriage drives, and went on seaside holidays at Weston-super-Mare. Church services were regularly held in a specially built chapel. The hospital grounds went down to the river, and Fox's Wood tunnel on the main line railway takes its name from the Fox family, who owned the wooded slopes through which the tunnel was driven. Two of Dr Fox's sons continued the work of the asylum.

The Quakers were active also in the moves to abolish the slave trade; some freed the slaves they owned themselves. Josiah Tucker, who held both the Deanery of Gloucester and the rectory of the mercantile parish of St Stephen's Bristol, was another opponent of the slave trade and plantation slavery. Most Bristol merchants, who owned slaves on their West Indies plantations, of course favoured the trade. But among the seamen who manned the slave ships there was opposition, not so much on the grounds of humanity but because of the high mortality among the white crews while they lay off the unhealthy coast of West Africa waiting for a cargo to be gathered for the 'middle passage'.

But Bristol, though deeply involved in the slave trade, seems never to have been England's chief slaving port, and as the century wore on it was far surpassed, in this as in other respects, by Liverpool. When, in 1786, the young clergyman Thomas Clarkson came to Bristol on his anti-slaving campaign he met some opposition, personally and in the local press, from plantation owners and slave dealers. But the Merchant Venturers, who knew the purpose of his visit, allowed him to search their records.

In a few more years Bristol's share in the slave trade had almost disappeared, and *Mathews' Directory* of 1793–4

Thomas Clarkson. His anti-slaving campaign brought him to Bristol as a young clergyman in 1786.

prided itself, from the moral standpoint, on Bristol's virtual abstention from the trade which had been 'nearly engrossed' by Liverpool. By the time the slave trade was formally abolished in 1807 Bristol no longer had any part in it.

Although the trade itself had been abolished, the owning of slaves in the West Indies continued till 1833, the year of emancipation. This final humanitarian move was a heavy blow to the West India interest, and threatened the devastation of trade links which were still important for Bristol when the whole economy of the city was in serious decline.

The Bristol Riots of 1831, though largely concerned with the need for Parliamentary Reform, also reflected the distress caused by this more general situation. The Bristol West India Association played its part, along with London, Glasgow, and Liverpool, in the campaign against the drastic step of emancipation. When this actually came the plantation owners received financial compensation for the loss of their slaves; the Baillies and the firm of T. and J. Daniel received the largest sums, but considerable compensation went to other slave-owning families.

The riots in the autumn of 1831 were a lurid, destructive episode in Bristol's history. They were partly sparked off by the nationwide agitation aroused by delays in passing the Reform Bill. The leaders of the Bristol Political Union were mainly concerned, as were those in similar organisations elsewhere, with this important issue; they had also called on the Corporation to resign and make way for an elected council. The arrival of Sir Charles Wetherell, the Recorder of Bristol, to open the Assizes was an extra provocation, as Sir Charles was a prominent and fanatical opponent of Parliamentary reform. Unrest of some kind was expected and as no proper police force existed a force of special constables was raised. Soldiers were also available should the situation get out of hand.

Disturbances started, on 29 October, when Wetherell entered the city. Those who took part in the riots were a mixed group, some educated and well dressed, but the

Queen Square in the riots of 1831.

majority were from the industrial areas in the centre and to the east of the city, uneducated and prone to violence. The authorities had at their head the mayor, Charles Pinney, a West India merchant. The cavalry were under the command not of an officer from any of their own regiments, but of Lt. Col. Brereton, who was Resident Inspecting Field Officer for the Bristol district and not an officer of any great military distinction.

Once rioting started the Bishop's Palace was burnt out, but a subsacrist barred a door and stopped the rioters from violating the cathedral. The new prison, built on the narrow strip of land between the New Cut and the Floating Harbour, was also much damaged. The main centre of rioting became Queen Square, where the Custom House on its northern side was gutted, and where the Mansion House was burnt out, with drunkenness among those who plundered the cellars. In the end Pinney, who was, in fact, sympathetic to the cause of reform, read the Riot Act and the troops who had been withdrawn from the city were called back, and suppressed the riot. At least twelve rioters were killed. Two sides of Queen Square had been gutted and had to be rebuilt; it was most fortunate that Rysbrack's splendid bronze statue of William III was undamaged.

The riots had been as much a protest against inefficient local government as a political demonstration; Bristol, unlike some rising northern or Midland industrial cities, already had its two Members of Parliament and a large body of people entitled to vote. The immediate sequel to the riots included the trial of Pinney and the court martial, early in 1832, of Brereton, whose home was in the district from which some of the rioters had come. Pinney was acquitted, but Brereton shot himself before the Court Martial could give its verdict. A few of the rioters were hanged, while others were imprisoned or transported. An interesting footnote to the proceedings was that furniture from the blazing Mansion House was saved by Isambard Kingdom Brunel and some friends who came down to see what help they could give to the forces of law and order. Brunel was then in Clifton, recovering his health after a bad accident in the Thames Tunnel, which had been designed by his father, Marc Isambard Brunel.

Nonconformist activity continued during the last years of the eighteenth century. The Unitarians built themselves a new chapel in Lewin's Mead of outstanding architectural quality, designed by William Blackburn from London. The Methodists now emerged as a separate

Mid-Victorian Bristol: Broad Street from St John's Arch.

denomination, notably after 1784 when John Wesley 'set apart', or ordained, ministers to replace those who had come back from their congregations in what were now the independent United States. Shortly before the end of the century, Captain Webb, who preached in the red coat of his regimentals, built the Portland Street Chapel on Kingsdown. The chapel had a bell in a small bellcote, emphasising the continuing closeness of the Methodists to the established Church. Other chapels, like that in Old King Street, were more what one came to expect in Nonconformist chapels.

Another religious body which now emerged from obscurity was that of the Catholics. Out at Baptist Mills the brassworks, run by Quakers who were more tolerant than most Bristolians at that time, brought in foreign workers from the Rhineland and what is now Belgium. Most of these immigrants were Catholics, and they demanded, as a condition of their employment, the freedom to practise their religion. The Quakers raised no objection. So a chapel was opened, and John Wesley remarked, in 1739, that at Baptist Mills many, if not most, of the inhabitants were Papists. In the central parishes Catholics were comparatively few, except in that of St Stephen, which had the harbour area within its parish and a congregation that included sailors and some Irish immigrants.

The priests who served the Bristol Catholics were mostly Jesuits from the 'College', or group of priests, of St Francis Xavier near Monmouth. The best known was Fr John Scudamore, a Jesuit who lived in Montague Street and was openly listed in *Sketchley's Directory* of 1775 as 'rev. R. priest'. By now, under the provisions of the Catholic Relief Act of 1778, which allowed Catholics to own property, a chapel had been opened in a warehouse in St James's parish. This was followed by the opening of the chapel in Trenchard Street. Refugee priests from France in the years after the French Revolution soon joined the Catholic clergy in Bristol and then, in 1834, a start was made on the classical church of the Apostles which later became the 'Pro' Cathedral of the Catholic diocese of Clifton.

In 1801 John Loudon McAdam, who was to be responsible for improving road transport throughout the country, came to live in Bristol. In 1811 he became the first president of the newly founded Commercial Coffee Rooms, whose Grecian building, by C.A. Busby, stood next to St Werburgh's church in Corn Street. Later, in 1823, he was a leading figure in the newly formed Chamber of Commerce. In 1815, having evolved his system of the macadamising of roads, he was appointed the Surveyor to the Bristol Turnpike Trust, so that the Bristol area became the first in the whole country to adopt the new, and markedly better system of road surfacing. McAdam was also a director of the London and Bristol Rail Road Company, and planned a railway, with a turnpike road alongside it, shorter than the Great Western line of a few years later. In the meantime the decay of Bristol's maritime trade continued, and caricatures were drawn of a fantastically derelict Floating Harbour, in which a rotting ship had a pennant saying that its owner had 'gone to Dr Fox's'.

Reform, the Port and Industry

The year 1832 included Parliamentary Reform, still leaving Bristol with two Members of Parliament. One of the 1832 Members was a Liberal, the other a strong Conservative, Sir Richard Vyvyan, who gave his name to Vyvyan Terrace in Clifton Park. This is the most impressive, Ionic-pillared of the Clifton terraces, started about 1835 and somewhat slowly finished. Vyvyan and another Tory were Members in 1835. Thereafter, till his death in 1870, the Hon. F.H.F. Berkeley sat as one of Bristol's two Liberals; he was a strong advocate of the secret ballot. From 1868 one of Bristol's M.P.s, induced to stand for the city by the Liberal Willses, was Samuel Morley, an advocate of temperance and of adult education, a music lover and prominent Congregationalist. He held the seat till 1885, the year when Bristol's Members were increased to four.

The year of Parliamentary Reform also saw some reorganisation in local government. Clifton and some outlying eastern areas came formally into the city, and it was divided into wards, with representation on the council by ward councillors. In 1835 the Municipal Corporations Act reorganised the charities, previously administered by the Corporation, and not always with the full income of those foundations going to educational or benevolent purposes. A new body, known as the Trustees of the Municipal Charities, was created. It administered some well-known almshouses, the bequests of such benefactors as Mrs Peloquin, who was of Huguenot origin, and the Grammar School, Queen Elizabeth's Hospital, and the Red Maids.

Those political and charitable improvements failed to resist the decline of the port, and the growing inadequacy of Bristol's up-river harbour. The Floating Harbour, with the water of the Frome flowing into it unimpeded, was silted up and severely polluted, but some relief came when the civil engineer William Chadwell Mylne laid a culvert, under Prince Street and then to the New Cut, to take the flow of Bristol's lesser river. Silting persisted in the main Floating Harbour, and this was relieved, at its lower end near the Cumberland Basin, by Brunel, who superintended the building of four low-level sluices which directed much of the silt into the lowermost reach of the New Cut. He also built the scraper dredges which helped to clean the Cumberland Basin, and in 1845 he reshaped one of the entrance locks so as to accommodate the curvature of ships' bottoms. But his idea for a deep-water pier at Portishead, which would remove the need for large ships to come up to the Floating Harbour, was never carried out.

The Bristol Docks Company, which had run the inner harbour since 1809, was severely hampered by the cost of the improvements which had been carried out and was unable to improve the harbour to the standards now required.

The suspension bridge over the Avon Gorge, scenically spectacular and potentially helpful in providing a new road access to northern Somerset and eventually to Portishead, was planned by Brunel in 1829, when it was wrongly assumed that the legacy made in 1753 by the vintner William Vick had accumulated enough money (at compound interest) for the building of a bridge across the gorge. Telford put forward a design which would have involved two colossal towers, rising from the floor of the

Isambard Kingdom Brunel, the nineteenth-century engineering genius.

Clifton Suspension Bridge, completed in 1864. By then, the Hot Well House (right) was well past its heyday.

gorge, to carry a suspension bridge of a strictly limited length. Brunel reckoned that, with the aid of a masonry abutment on the Somerset side, a single span of 630 feet would provide the answer. The design included 'pylons', which would enshrine the pseudo-Egyptian style then popular; these were to have sphinxes on their tops.

Brunel's scheme was accepted in 1830, ground was broken on the Clifton side in 1831, but financial difficulties, and the deterrent effect of the Riots, caused a delay of five years. In 1836 work was resumed, and the laying of the foundation stone was ceremonially carried out during the visit of the British Association. But money soon ran out, the whole of Vick's augmented legacy had been spent, and work ground to a halt for over twenty years. The Clifton Suspension Bridge, perhaps the greatest single

adornment of the Bristol scene, was not finished till 1864, and then as a memorial to its designer, who had died in 1859.

With the end, in 1834, of the East India Company's monopoly of the tea trade, some ports outside London, including Bristol and Liverpool, hoped to engage in this business. The finest of all Bristol's dockside warehouses, at the bottom of Prince Street, a subtle blend of grey pennant stone and Bath-stone dressings, was extended by 1837 to include storage space for tea and the relevant auction rooms. The designer was the prolific local architect Richard Shackleton Pope. But 'outports' like Bristol could not compete with London's expertise in the tea trade, and this impressive building, commandingly sited at the junction of the Avon and Frome arms of the Floating

Harbour, soon reverted to general warehousing, and became known as the Bush warehouse. Its imaginative conversion in the 1970s to house the Arnolfini contemporary arts centre and offices was a pioneering reuse of redundant dockside buildings.

Across the water from the Bush warehouse two modern transit sheds, built at a time when moderate-sized ships still came into the Floating Harbour, have replaced those bombed in the war. One now houses the city's industrial museum. A plaque explains that here was the site of Patterson's shipyard, from which, in 1837, the hull of Brunel's *Great Western* was launched; a paddle-steamer,

she was the largest ship built in Bristol at the time. By then steamships were often seen in the Floating Harbour; most of them were packet boats on the Irish run or maintaining services to ports on the Bristol Channel. They needed coal, and Bristol's earliest railways were laid down to connect the harbours with the collieries to the north-east of the city.

The first of these railways was the Bristol and Gloucestershire, started in 1828 and completed, to a point in the Floating Harbour, in 1835. It brought coal from near Westerleigh and Coalpit Heath to steamers in the harbour. A railway, or tramway, with a similar coal-carrying

Brunel's great Temple Meads railway terminus was started in 1836.

Lithograph by J.C. Bourne (1842) showing the magnificent interior of Temple Meads.

purpose was the Avon and Gloucestershire, coming down to the Avon near Keynsham, and with two branches, one of which could add to the coal supplies of Bristol, while the other could, by means of the navigable Avon, supplement stocks in Bath.

The 'Great Western', or London and Bristol, Railway was authorised by Act of Parliament in 1835. It was 'begun to be dug' in the following year. At first Temple Meads was a broad-gauge station, and the line was continued westward by the Bristol and Exeter – like the Great Western a broad-gauge line – engineered by Brunel and coming in at right angles to the Great Western, so that passengers travelling further west had to change trains. Eventually a curved track connected the two railways, and the Bristol and Exeter and the G.W.R. were merged in 1876. The goods station was originally at a lower level, on the northern side, with lifts to carry the freight wagons up or down, and a camber for barges using the Floating Harbour. Brunel's original station was a fine essay in the Perpendicular Gothic of about 1500; it was used by the Midland, or L.M.S. trains, and more recently by the Exploratory Science Museum and the developing Museum of Empire and Commonwealth.

Other railways completing the complex converging on Bristol included the Bristol and South Wales. This at first ran out from the shore on a long pier at New Passage, thus connecting with the South Wales trains which ran from another pier on the Gwent side. Only the opening, in 1886, of the Severn Tunnel allowed for an unimpeded run from Bristol to Newport or Cardiff. The Portishead line, down the Somerset side of the gorge, came in the 1860s, to make a link with Portishead Dock, and in 1873 the line to connect Bristol and the Somerset coal mines, with its spectacular viaduct at Pensford, was opened. Another railway, running along the Bristol side of the gorge, was the Port and Pier, built to connect the port of Bristol – in other words the city docks and the Floating Harbour – and the pier, which ran out, at the mouth of the Avon, near the site of the later Avonmouth Dock. The Port and Pier railway was always short of money and although it connected, by means of the tunnel under the Downs, with the Midland Railway, no passenger trains were let through that tunnel till 1885.

In shipbuilding, the next major event was the building of a ship considerably larger than the *Great Western*, for the transatlantic run. First known as the *Mammoth*, then the *Leviathan*, but completed as the *Great Britain*, she was at first to have been a paddle-ship; but Brunel changed her design to that of a screw steamer. Her gross tonnage was nearly three thousand, and when finished in 1845, she was the largest ship in the world. Her iron hull had clipper bows, and, apart from her engines, there were six masts, which gave her a schooner rig.

The *Great Britain* had a varied career, starting on the transatlantic service out of Liverpool. In 1846 she was stranded in Dundrum Bay in Northern Ireland, and although she was refloated next year the effort and the expense bankrupted the Great Western Steamship company and the ship was sold. The most successful

Two of Brunel's great ships were launched from Bristol dockyards: the Great Western *(left) and the* Great Britain.

part of her career was as an emigrant ship to Australia. Eventually she had her engines taken out, and her last voyages round Cape Horn to California were as a three-masted sailing ship. On one of these voyages she was damaged by a serious gale, returned to the Falkland Isles where, as a 'constructive derelict', she functioned as a coal store and as a wool warehouse in the harbour of Port Stanley. But in 1970, perched on a pontoon and towed across the Atlantic, the *Great Britain* came back to Bristol, and is now, under continuous restoration in the dock in which she was built, one of the prime sights of the city.

The difficulty of getting the *Great Britain* through the outer set of locks into the tidal Avon in the 1840s, and the wreck in 1851 of the *Demerara*, a wooden paddle-steamer nearly as large as the *Great Britain*, showed how unsuitable Bristol's up-river harbour was for use by the larger steamships of the nineteenth century. Liverpool, already used by the four first ships of the Cunard Line, which provided a regular shuttle service across the Atlantic, was clearly more suitable as a transatlantic port. The only solution for Bristol was the building of docks at, or near, the mouth of the Avon.

The Free Port Association had, in 1848, succeeded in getting great reductions in dues on goods unloaded in the Floating Harbour, which was still effectively the Port of Bristol. The City Docks were thus made over to the Corporation, and the Free Port Association for a time absorbed the Chamber of Commerce. This freeing of the Port increased the volume of traffic, but there was soon agitation for port facilities – for larger ships unable to navigate the gorge – at the point where the Avon joined the Severn estuary. These endeavours were set afoot by rival groups of private developers. A new dock at Avonmouth was finished in 1877 and one at Portishead two years later. But considerable traffic, of sailing ships and of moderately sized steamers, still came up the Gorge to the historic City Docks, and Bristol long kept the distinctive character of a town in which seagoing ships, some of them of about 3000 tons, could be seen in the very midst of the city.

Shipbuilding continued in the centre of Bristol. Hill's, who also ran the Bristol City line of steamers, built ships in their Albion yard on the southern side of the Floating Harbour. They and Patterson's both built small gunboats for service against Russia in the Crimean War. Stothert's, sometimes called Stothert and Slaughter's, built iron ships, while the Clift House shipyard launched ships diagonally, at high tide, into the lowermost part of the New Cut; this shipyard, under the name of Payne's, continued till 1923. Nor far away an Australian House Manufactory built prefabricated houses, shops, and even churches, for use in the newly opened goldfields in Australia.

Bristol continued, in the nineteenth century, as an industrial city; the keynote of this activity was its great variety. The chief figure in Bristol's coal industry, with scientific and correct ideas on the geology of the mines on the Gloucestershire side of the city, was Handel Cossham, who owned several pits in that part of the coalfield. He was also Mayor of Bath, where he had a house, and was a Liberal Member of Parliament for Bristol for five years. There were also coal mines on the southern side of Bristol, in Bedminster and out as far as South Liberty and Malago Vale.

Out in Kingswood, another industry grew up as a by-product of coal mining. Retired or disabled miners repaired or made heavy boots for miners, agricultural workers, and quarrymen; they worked at home or as outworkers from more extensive workshops. Factory production, on a larger scale but still with some outworking, came after 1850, while in the city itself more general footwear was produced by Derham's, who employed about two thousand workers in the 1880s, and by other firms. In Kingswood itself, once mining had ceased, several bootmakers flourished and made up the leading local industry. Many of those who ran bootmaking firms were also prominent in Methodism, which was the main religious denomination in Kingswood, with over forty chapels for various and competing aspects of Methodism.

Another industry, with one very large mill in the area of Barton Hill, was cotton spinning. The Great Western Cotton works received their first bales of American cotton when the *Great Western* came back from the United States. The company had been formed in 1836, and the mill, which was one of England's largest, was built by the end of 1838. All through the nineteenth century the firm had some fifteen hundred workers, with many people coming from Lancashire to set up the initial labour force. The closure of the cotton works came in the 1920s; the castellated mill survived for some years as a transport depot but has now been pulled down.

Sugar refining of the traditional type declined in Bristol about the time of the abolition of slavery. But steam refining, with sugar bought from various places, continued under the control of Conrad Finzel, a German immigrant who came to Bristol in 1836 and established his business near the southern side of Bristol Bridge. The refinery, with about five hundred workers, was among the largest in the country, and lasted till 1877. Finzel also built himself a large neo-Elizabethan house at Clevedon as a seaside summer home.

Soap-making, a Bristol industry going back many centuries, flourished in the nineteenth century. The leading firm, eventually merged with Lever Brothers, was that of Christopher Thomas, whose 'Puritan' washing soap was first manufactured in 1898, and whose medieval Italianate factory in Broad Plain was a striking piece of architecture that has somewhat wrongly been styled as Bristol Byzantine. Thomas himself was of Welsh origin, became Mayor of Bristol and was the first mayor to live, during his year of office, in the donated Mansion House facing Clifton Down. His own house was neo-Elizabethan in style and stood, on the edge of what was then the countryside, in Durdham Park.

The tobacco and chocolate trades were still important in a city largely concerned with the output of consumer goods; to a large extent, the growing engineering industry existed to supply the technical needs of those firms. Chocolate-making in Bristol grew as chocolate developed as a sweet as well as a drink. Fry's, who had a thousand employees in the 1880s, were joined in the industry by another firm, Packer's, who built a large factory, close to the Midland Railway, in the Greenbank district, they also had a factory under the name of Carson's at Mangotsfield. Fry's remained close to the middle of the old city; not till after the First World War, when they amalgamated with Cadbury's (another Quaker concern in an industry almost a Quaker preserve), did they move out to Keynsham.

In the tobacco industry the Wills family eventually became dominant, and when, in 1901, the Imperial Tobacco Company was formed smaller local firms such as Franklyn Davey's and Edwards Ringer and Bigg became part of the great combine; Ringer's operated from a striking Italianate factory in Redcliffe Street. In 1886 Wills

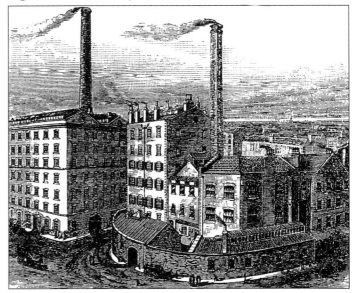

Fry's chocolate factory, Nelson Street, Bristol.

moved to a new factory, with Victorian Gothic touches of design, in East Street, Bedminster, a mere barrow-push away from the coal mine in Dean Lane (Bedminster mines were increasingly important for industry in that part of Bristol). Wills built a new factory on another site in Bedminster in 1900. Sir W.H. Wills, later Lord Winterstoke, was largely concerned in 1901 with the creation of Imperial Tobacco, to defend the British industry against competition in the home market from the British and American Tobacco Company. By now the chief production of Wills was in cigarettes, with the Bonsack cigarette-making machine introduced from the United States becoming a powerful factor in the success of the newly named firm.

Packaging was a natural process in a city so much engaged in the manufacture of consumer goods. The firm which met many of those needs was E.S. and A. Robinson. The Robinson family originated in the Forest of Dean. They were Baptists and eventually built the new Baptist College behind the University. The first Elisha Smith Robinson arrived in Bristol in 1844, and built a factory at the top end of Redcliffe Street, for the manufacture of wrapping paper and paper bags. The firm later expanded into Bedminster, and long remained a largely family enterprise.

In 1884 the three dock systems – in the City, at Avonmouth, and Portishead – came under unified civic control. A new dock office, in a Victorian Renaissance style and dated 1885, was built in Queen Square. There remained, for the rest of the century, the problem of the improvement of the central docks and of the approach up the tidal river. This included the sharp controversy between those who supported 'dockisation', this being the conversion of the Avon, all down its length, into a tide-free harbour.

What the 'dockisers' proposed was the building of a dam, near Avonmouth, which would free the Avon from the rise and fall of the tide. What the 'dockisers' did not do was to suggest a straight cut through the Horseshoe bend, near Shirehampton, which would make it possible for ships about 400 feet long to come up to the middle of the city. Another scheme proposed that the lock should be not far from the Horseshoe bend itself. A new entrance lock into Cumberland Basin, long enough to take the ships now envisaged, was opened in 1873. But as the obstacle of the Horseshoe bend was never removed a restriction of about 330 feet in length remained. So no really large ships ever used the new lock, and it often contained two, or even three, small ships at once. The Floating Harbour, and the City Docks, still remained important for coasters and short-sea traders. The last years before 1900 still saw schemes, of engineering and architectural note, for the improvement of port facilities in what was still known, from the medieval building which had once been St Augustine's Abbey of Canons Regular, as Canons Marsh.

The last new industrial buildings in the City Docks, put up about 1900, were along one side of St Augustine's Reach, and opposite Narrow Quay. Transit sheds were built, and railway lines were laid down for Great Western goods trains; the Midland preferred barges to link their trains with ships in the Floating Harbour. The edges of the new quays were built of finely cut granite and the northern end of the last transit shed was ornamentally treated by Edward Gabriel, a competent architect in the 'Arts and Crafts' tradition. It is a pity that the detail of his embellishment, meant to be admired by those crossing what was still called the Tramways Centre, has worn so badly. All future port developments in the port of Bristol were to be at Avonmouth, which was now included within the city's boundaries. The Royal Edward Dock was started in 1902 and was opened by King Edward VII in July 1908.

Victorian Religion, Arts and Education

An ecclesiastical episode that occurred soon after the Reform Act of 1832 in some ways reflected the controversy which accompanied that political event. The bishops, who at that time automatically had seats in the House of Lords, had mostly opposed reform. As new bishoprics were being created to serve industrial areas in the North, the Whig, or Liberal, Government felt that the number of bishoprics should be restricted. So in 1836 the diocese of Bristol, its Dorset territory having been returned to Salisbury, was merged with that of Gloucester. The diocese, like the medieval diocese of Bath and Wells, was a genuinely double one, with two cathedrals, two deaneries, and two chapters.

By no means all the Anglicans in Bristol happily accepted these developments. The first move was the enlargement of the cathedral to a size, not of such major cathedrals as York or Canterbury, but equivalent to smaller cathedrals such as Rochester. So the 'Cinderella' status of Bristol Cathedral was eased by the building of a new nave, similar in character to the choir limb, with the aisles as tall as the middle alleyway. The architect was G.E. Street, and the main work was finished in 1877, with the western towers, giving the cathedral an impressive three-towered silhouette, put up a few years later. The revival of the diocese itself, favoured by Gladstone, who much admired the memory of Bishop Butler and edited his works, came in 1897. The boundaries of the new bishopric included Bristol itself, the southernmost tip of Gloucestershire and northern Wiltshire.

Church building continued in a city which was still growing, despite economic and port troubles. Some old and small churches were replaced by substantial Victorian buildings, as happened at Stapleton and Bedminster; both these new churches were by John Norton, who also designed Emmanuel Church in Clifton and the fine tower and spire of Christ Church in Clifton. The construction of Christ Church started in the 1840s and it was given this crowning feature, whose pinnacle is one of the highest points in Bristol, in 1859. G.E. Street was the chief architect of All Saints' in Pembroke Road, always a High Church place of worship, as were some other new churches in Bristol. More than forty churches, new or replacements for older buildings, were built in the nineteenth century or soon after 1900.

The Nonconformists were active church-builders, too. A few of their new buildings, like the handsome Ionic Brunswick Chapel in Brunswick Square, were classical; the Kensington Chapel, by an architect from Glasgow, also has an excellent Grecian façade. It replaced an earlier chapel on the same site, and dates from the 1880s. Other Nonconformist churches were of the 'tabernacle' type, often Romanesque in character. Gothic of a more pronounced type was used by the Congregationalists in several chapels, in Sneyd Park, Cotham, Clifton, Bishopston, and elsewhere. The Congregationalists were, socially speaking, the élite among Bristol's Nonconformists and they seem deliberately to have used the style of the Victorian churches put up by the established Church.

The churchyards of the central churches were by now severely congested, and the 1830s coincided with the early stages of the movement to establish cemeteries which would be less overcrowded, and more hygienic, than the existing graveyards, described as 'dangerous masses of corruption'. The first of such cemeteries, in London, was at Kensal Green; Marc Isambard Brunel was on its committee. A committee came into being in Bristol and included some of those who had been concerned with the building of the *Great Western*. The first site suggested was in Ashley Vale, but was later changed to Arno's Vale on the way to Brislington. The scene was more rural than it is now, and the prospect recalled the Valley of the Arno in Tuscany. The site was first intended for the Bristol Zoo, but when this was started at Clifton instead, Arno's Vale became available for burials. The enabling Act of Parliament was passed in 1837. Work soon started and the Anglican part of the cemetery was consecrated by Bishop Monk in 1840.

The unconsecrated part of the cemetery could be used for Nonconformist and other funerals; some of the Willses and Robinsons were buried there, and the upper path, commanding a fine view over the supposedly Florentine landscape, leads past the graves of many people who were prominent in Victorian Bristol. The entrance lodges and the chapel next to the present crematorium are impeccably Grecian – Doric or Ionic – while the chapel built for Anglican funerals is Renaissance Italianate, and a building of some quality. In the late 1990s, public opinion thwarted the attempt by its private owners to close the cemetery.

The best-known monument in the cemetery is that of the Indian social reformer Raja Ram Mohun Roy, who died at Stapleton in 1833 while on a visit to Bristol. He was an associate of the local Unitarians, and went to services in the Chapel in Lewin's Mead. Eleven years later he was buried in the Nonconformist section of the cemetery at Arno's Vale. His monument, put up by a grandfather of Rabindranath Tagore, was by an English architect but is of strongly Indian character, with *chattris* and other Indian features. A second statue was erected outside Bristol's Central Library in 1997.

Bristol's charities continued to do their work, some-times in an expanded form; some of the older ones had more scope now that they were controlled by the trustees of the Municipal Charities. Of the new, one of the most notable was that founded, for orphans, by the German George Muller. He started on a small scale, near Portland Square, but later moved up to Ashley Down, where his group of grim, barrack-like blocks came to house hundreds of orphans from all parts of the country. The windows were placed too high for children to see out, and the regime was so restrictive that the orphans, when placed in jobs, displayed little initiative. Muller had been a pastor in Germany, and the group to which he now became affiliated was that of the Plymouth Brethren. Three times a day the orphans marched, behind a band, to the Bethesda Chapel at the top of Great George Street, and this became one of the more notable sights of the city. Muller died, aged ninety-two, in 1898.

Another local charity was the pioneering girls' reformatory school established, in the Red Lodge in Park Row, by Mary Carpenter, the renowned Unitarian. The poet Byron's widow bought the building to serve Mary

Mary Carpenter set up, in 1854, the country's first girls' reformatory school at Bristol's Red Lodge.

Carpenter's charitable purpose. Here, as in the orphan houses, there was a somewhat grim regime. Another woman philanthropist in Bristol was Susanna Winkworth, a sister of Catherine Winkworth, the translator of German hymns, who also played a part in educational moves in Bristol. Susanna Winkworth was, for a time, a Unitarian and certainly knew Mary Carpenter. She started a company for the better housing of manual workers; this was at a time when there were still no council houses. In 1875 the company put up the Jacobs Wells Industrial Dwellings, severely 'Scotch Baronial' in style, with crow-stepped gables to give extra character to the tenements.

Medicine continued to develop in Victorian Bristol, with a curious political alignment of the two leading hospitals. The Bristol Royal Infirmary was mainly supported by Conservative benefactors. The Bristol General Hospital – started in 1832 in Guinea Street, off Redcliffe Hill, and moved in 1858 to the pseudo Jacobean building, with large lettable cellars beneath it, which overlooks Bathurst Basin – was mainly supported by Liberals, so that events to raise money for it became Liberal social occasions.

A leading medical man in early Victorian Bristol was Dr James Cowles Prichard, of partly Quaker origin. He came to Bristol in 1810, was a physician at the Infirmary, and allied by marriage to the local Unitarians. He became an expert in the treatment of insanity, and lived in the Red Lodge before it became Mary Carpenter's Reformatory School.

Dr John Addington Symonds was a physician at the General Hospital, and a Liberal. He lived in the fine early Georgian mansion of Clifton Hill House. Originally from Oxford, he was a lecturer in the Bristol Medical School, which was a forerunner of the University of Bristol, had a large private practice, and in 1863 became President of the British Medical Association. His son, of the same name as his father, was for a long time Bristol's leading man of letters.

Some more almshouses, in addition to the large number already existing in Bristol, were founded during the nineteenth century. The 'Queen Anne' design of Bengough's in Horfield Road was influenced by Colston's Almhouse just behind it. The range of the Haberfield almshouses commanded a fine view of ships coming in or out of the Floating Harbour.

Though Clifton was now within the city of Bristol, it was still non-commercial and very different in character from other parts of Bristol. Its residents were largely retired people, including army and naval officers, university (i.e. Oxford or Cambridge) graduates, retired clergy and families with some aristocratic connections. Such

The Assembly Rooms, built in 1806 by F.H. Greenway for Clifton's polite society, also served as a hotel for visitors to the resort.

Interior of the Assembly Rooms, painted in the early nineteenth century by Rolinda Sharples.

people could help to initiate new educational foundations. The political sympathies of Clifton were Conservative, so that when the Zoological Gardens opened in 1836, with their fine terrace and entrance lodges facing the Downs, they became the scene of Conservative outdoor social events.

The Victoria Rooms, projected in William IV's reign and started in 1838 by Charles Dyer, were long known as the Victoria Conservative Rooms. The Rooms were opened in 1842 and the Liberal papers wrote scornfully on the proceedings. Any gatherings held in the public rooms must have been Conservative, but cultural events included recitals by Jenny Lind, readings by Dickens and Oscar Wilde, and piano recitals by Paderewski.

Bristol claims a place in the history of the cinema as the birthplace of William Friese-Greene, who was born in College Street in 1855. He was first named William Green, but added Friese to his name when he married a Swiss lady named Helena Friese. He went to the City School, became the apprentice of a photographer in Queen's Road, had a studio in Bath, and in a house in Clifton did

The Victoria Rooms in more leisurely times, before the swirl of modern traffic.

experimental work which led to his pioneering work on the cinema. Experts still disagree as to the significance of his contribution.

The Theatre Royal, in the by now unsalubrious dock-lands, was no longer fashionable in the mid-Victorian period; a return from it, in those days of horse-drawn carriages, was uphill and tedious. Most of its patrons tended to live in Clifton or other residential suburbs. So in 1866 James Henry Chute, a son-in-law of William Macready, bought a site in Park Row and there built the New Theatre Royal, which was opened in 1867. Its architect was the renowned theatre designer Charles J. Phipps, and he used a mixture of styles for what soon became Bristol's most fashionable theatre, normally known as The Prince's. In 1902 it was redecorated and newly furnished; the architect for the work was another well-known theatre architect, Frank Matcham. The building was destroyed in the Second World War.

It was not surprising, in view of its scenery both above and below the city, that nineteenth-century Bristol saw the rise of a considerable school of landscape painters. The Frome and Avon valleys, especially the scenery of the Avon Gorge, contained many 'Romantic' subjects, more dramatic than the views near Norwich which inspired the Norwich School of painters. Leading artists among the Bristol School included Francis Danby, an Irishman who settled in Bristol and had two artist sons; among his pupils were Samuel Jackson and John Baker Pyne, an artist with a delicate touch. Others included Paul Falconer Poole, who became a prominent Royal Academician, and two artists named Fripp, who were grandsons of Nicholas Pocock, the maritime artist and former ship's captain. Joseph Walter was another marine artist who did paintings of the *Great Western* and other vivid nautical scenes.

More unusual, and of note for his rich use of colour, was William James Muller. His German father came to Bristol as a refugee from Napoleonic rule. William was helped by members of the intellectual élite, including the Carpenters and Dean Beeke. His travels in the Near East helped his fine sense of colour, but they also affected his health and he died in Bristol in 1845. Another Bristol artist was Rolinda Sharples, the daughter of James Sharples who produced many accurate pastel portraits, in America and in Bath and Bristol. Rolinda Sharples painted graphic and accurate views of racing on the Downs and of the trial of Col. Brereton after the riots of 1831. She died young, but a gift of money from her mother helped in the building of the West of England Academy, which opened in 1858.

Education, in the days before compulsory teaching in board schools, was privately organised, at home by tutors and governesses, and in private academies like that on St Michael's Hill run by the scholarly local historian the Revd Samuel Seyer, who also held the living of Horfield. Private tutors, and governesses, were a leading element in middle-class society.

The ancient endowed schools now went through a varied and chequered time. The Cathedral School, undamaged in the riot of 1831, during which the Bishop's Palace was wrecked and the cathedral was threatened, continued as a diocesan school for the training of school-masters, but when this was abolished it went back to its earlier function. Colston's School was still in the Elizabethan Great House, but moved to a semi-rural site at Stapleton. The Grammar School, by now on its site in Unity Street, was still in an unsatisfactory state, and Queen Elizabeth's Hospital (the City School) was not much helped by its move, in 1847, to its new site on Brandon Hill. The Red Maids' School, despite its new buildings finished early in the 1840s, was not in a pros-perous state. In 1879 the Grammar School solved many of its problems by moving uphill to a large Gothic building in Tyndall's Park.

It was no surprise that efforts were made to establish schools, of a 'public school' type, which could provide boys with a better education than that available in the old endowed schools. Two new schools reflected the religious controversy between Nonconformists and the Church of England.

Bristol College, in rented buildings in Park Row, was planned in 1829. A leading figure behind the project was Dr J.C. Prichard. Theological teaching was to be in accor-dance with the doctrines of the Church of England, but only for pupils who might desire it. Nonconformists were also to be admitted. The college opened, with only thirty pupils, in 1831, but the Anglican clergy in Bristol, from Bishop Gray downwards, were hostile, and it closed in 1841. The Bishop's College, started in buildings meant for the Red Maids near the top of Park Street, was started by Bishop Monk in 1840 as a strictly Anglican foundation. But it was never a financial success, and it closed in 1861, a year before the foundation of the more durable Clifton College.

Another college, in this case for the training of women teachers in church schools, was a foundation for which Bishop Monk was largely responsible. It opened under the name of St Matthias in 1853.

In 1860 Clifton College started, as did many new places of education founded in those days, in the drawing room of one of those responsible for its foundation: H.S. Wasbrough; the Mayor of Bristol was in the chair. The Clifton College Company was formed, and a council, whose chairman was Canon Guthrie, was appointed. Land was bought, the buildings were designed by Charles Hansom, and the college was opened in 1862. From the start, in so residential a district as Clifton, many day boys (known as Town Boys) were admitted. The first effective headmaster was John Percival, who had been at Rugby; in seventeen years he made Clifton one of England's leading public schools and built up an outstanding staff. His polit-ical and theological views were liberal, and he became friendly with some leading Nonconformist ministers. An innovative feature was a boarding house for Jewish boys. One of the masters in Percival's time was T.E. Brown, best known as a leading Manx man of letters, and among notable pupils at the school was Henry Newbolt, later to inspire a nation with poems like 'Vitai Lampada', with its stirring exhortation to 'Play up! Play up! and play the game!'

Girls' education, in day schools, also took on a new impetus in the Victorian period. In 1876 the possibility of establishing a high school for girls was discussed. A committee was formed which included John Percival and some Bristol business men. Clifton High School was incorporated in 1877 and opened in 1878; it was to override distinctions of class and religious denominations. It moved to another building a year later. It had a cricket team, in which two daughters of W.G. Grace played. Shortly afterwards, in 1880, Redland High School opened; it later moved from the small premises it occupied to the fine Georgian mansion of Redland Court.

Most children in Bristol were still taught in church schools or, after the Education Act of 1870, in the board schools, of which many were built between then and the end of the century. The School Boards, some of them started before such areas as Horfield came into the City of Bristol, to some extent corresponded to the urban districts as first set up. By 1888, when the county councils came into being, attendance at school had been made compulsory.

An important figure in Bristol's cultural life at this time was the younger John Addington Symonds, son of the well-known doctor of the same name. He went to Balliol College at Oxford, where he became a Fellow of Magdalen, and after the death of his father in 1871 lived in Clifton Hill House. He gave lectures both at Clifton College and at the classes started by Catherine Winkworth, of the Committee for the Higher Education of Women. Having never openly acknowledged 'The Problem' (his homosexuality), he spent his last years at Davos in Switzerland, because of his consumption. He was still in Bristol when he took part in moves which led, in 1876, to the foundation of the University College.

The 'Oxbridge' monopoly of England's university education was broken as the nineteenth century progressed. Durham and London got their universities, and Manchester and Newcastle had university colleges which later became fully chartered universities. At Bristol the Medical School already existed as one of the University's later components, and the Trade School, which later became the Trade and Mining School, became the Engineering Faculty of the university.

Preliminary moves, by Percival and others, culminated in an historic meeting held in the Victoria Rooms on 11 June 1874. The mayor presided, and many of Bristol's intellectual élite were present, among them John Addington Symonds, Catherine Winkworth, Mary Carpenter, Samuel Morley, the Dean of Bristol, and John Percival. Guest speakers included William Temple, the Bishop of Exeter (later Archbishop of Canterbury), Mary Carpenter's brother, who was the Registrar of the University of London, the historian E.G. Freeman, author of a history of Bristol, and the Warden of New College at Oxford. The most important guest speaker was Benjamin Jowett, the Master of Balliol. He urged that any university college started in Bristol should add liberal and literary instruction to its more technical courses.

One of the main purposes of this meeting was to raise money for the proposed University College. Balliol and New College both contributed; so too did Lewis Fry of the chocolate firm; of the Wills family, the future Lord Winterstoke sent a letter of support. Members of the British Association, whose meeting of 1875 was held in Bristol, gave some support, and in 1876 the University College opened modestly in two Georgian houses in Park Row. It had more students at evening classes than day students, and from the beginning admitted women. Its first buildings were in a three-sided court, designed by Charles Hansom, facing out towards the new Grammar School, and its first principal was the eminent economist Alfred Marshall, whose wife was also on the staff.

University College, Bristol, started reasonably well, though student numbers were modest and the local prestige of the college was low. Money was also short and

Homage to John Ruskin and the Venetian Gothic: Foster & Ponton's Philosophical Institution, which after completion in 1871 was called the Bristol Museum and Library, is now a café-bar.

lecturers, who received poor salaries, were apt to combine several subjects. One activity, appropriate for a college whose scope included Somerset, was the establishment, in 1904, of the National Fruit and Cider Institute, which later became the Department of Agriculture and Horticulture in the chartered university.

In 1899 a University College 'Colston' society was formed to raise money to hold annual dinners and to raise money for the college. In 1906, £30,000 was given by Fry and Wills donors, to go towards the college's endowment. It was at a dinner held in 1908 that the third Henry Overton Wills promised to give £100,000 towards the endowment of a university, provided that a Charter was granted within two years. John Percival, now in the House of Lords as Bishop of Hereford, helped in Parliament and the city of Bristol made a grant from the rates. The Charter was granted in 1909, and the university coat of arms, including the flaming sun of the Wills family, came in the same year. The first new buildings, largely faced with attractive pink pennant stone, were soon built, the architect being George Oatley.

The Early Twentieth Century

The Royal Edward Dock opened in 1908, in time to play a vital role in the First World War, as the Bristol Channel was not much penetrated by German submarines. Avonmouth was thus of very great service, from 1917 onwards, for the unloading of military equipment and supplies from the United States; the City Docks also played their part in this process. Between the wars the Royal Edward Dock was twice expanded northwards. The new western arm, which became the oil arm for tankers, was built between 1919 and 1922. Most of the eastern arm, for use by general cargo ships, was built between 1922 and 1928, but a final enlargement was not finished till 1940.

Bristol's great new industry, at Filton, just north of the city boundary, was the manufacture of aircraft. The British and Colonial Aircraft Company started work in 1910. Its founder, Sir George White, had built up an important business on the electrification of tramways, including those of Bristol. The aircraft firm was started with Sir George's own money. Production, with a few orders from the War Office, more from the Admiralty and some from abroad, was still small before the outbreak of the First World War; at that time there were only about four hundred employees at Filton, and some at Brislington. Aircraft production increased greatly during the war, in particular on the Bristol Scout and on the Bristol Fighter. Just after the war the firm's name became The Bristol Aeroplane Company (BAC); aeronautical work, on seaplanes, was also carried out at nearby Yate.

Shortly after the war there were changes in BAC when the firm acquired the Cosmos Engineering Company and

Sir George White, champion of Britain's emerging aeronautical industry and founder of what became British Aerospace.

set up its engineering division, with its works at Patchway, and so built aero-engines as well as the aircraft

Early aircraft from BAC's Filton works: the Bristol Boxkite, built in 1910, and a Bristol Bulldog showing its paces (174 mph) in 1927.

frames. During some of the inter-war years the engine division was more prosperous than BAC, which produced aircraft, and the Bristol Bulldog, a leading fighter with the Royal Air Force, was both built and engined at Filton and Patchway. But work increased with the impetus of re-armament, and BAC's Blenheim was valued both as a bomber and as a fighter.

As the Second World War went on the aircraft industry, widely dispersed with some production at Weston-super-Mare and in the underground stone mines at Corsham, became the chief source of employment in Bristol, with the Beaufighter one of its most important aircraft. Aircraft were also imported from the United States; some of them, fully assembled, were towed with wings outstretched up the Portway, which connected Avonmouth and central Bristol. The Portway was itself a fine new highway along one side of the Avon Gorge, replacing, on part of its track, the Port and Pier Railway, which had closed in 1922.

Bristol's industrial activity was still extremely varied, thus lessening the degree of unemployment in the city, compared to what occurred in South Wales. Shipbuilding

continued in Hill's Albion Dockyard, on merchant ships and also on naval tonnage. Ships for the Royal Navy included corvettes, frigates, and small landing craft. A new industry, created during the First World War to produce zinc, which had almost become a German and Belgian monopoly, was the National Smelting Corporation. In its large works, built in the flat country north of Avonmouth, sulphuric acid was also produced.

At the other side of Bristol widely varied industry grew up in the new trading estate at Brislington. On the outskirts of Keynsham, a large new chocolate factory was built by Fry's after its merger with Cadbury's; the factory in the midst of the city which made the nearby streets redolent of chocolate was abandoned and turned over to other uses.

Imperial Tobacco continued production in its Bedminster factories. This was on a massive scale and resulted in great wealth for various members of the Wills family, whose lavish benefactions transformed the Bristol University. The main building, now known as the Wills Memorial Building, which had been planned before the

Arts and Crafts flamboyance in Edward Everard's printing works of 1900.

Etching by Gwendoline Cross of the University Tower, designed by Sir George Oatley and completed in the 1920s.

war, was now finished, and was opened by George V in 1925; the designer was Sir George Oatley. The noble tower, 215 feet high including its lantern, rises at the top of Park Street and is now, from many viewpoints, an essential landmark of Bristol. Its splendid fan-vaulted hall leads to a Great Hall of assembly, a reception room, lecture rooms, a library and rooms for members of staff. The building was the joint gift of Sir George Wills and Henry Herbert Wills. Up the hill, and on part of the site of Prince Rupert's

Royal Fort, the Henry Herbert Wills Physics Laboratory was built in the 1920s, castellated with four corner turrets and an un-Gothic array of fluted Ionic pilasters. The Grammar School, not far away, had a new classroom wing which was the gift of Lord Winterstoke. Wills Hall, yet another family benefaction, was the most impressive of the university's halls of residence.

Bristol has a long history of benefactions from its great business families. One spectacular twentieth-century charity – founded by Henry Herbert Wills, and his wife Dame Monica Wills – was at Westbury-on-Trym, on a fine site at the far end of Durdham Down. This was St Monica's Home of Rest, providing for ladies suffering from chronic illness, who had to be of 'gentle birth' and Anglicans preferably of a High Church outlook. The buildings, started before Henry Herbert Wills' death in 1922, were finished in 1925. They were on a lavish scale and cost over £600,000. They included a splendid chapel in the Perpendicular style, though the other blocks, among them a separate building put up as a nurses' home, were Jacobean in character. They were set in fine gardens, and were most thoughtfully planned both for administration and for the comfortable accommodation of the residents, who at first numbered sixty. The trustees of the home's finances are the Merchant Venturers.

The years between the wars saw great expansion in local authority housing. Many areas were developed in this way, with brick-built, two-storey houses of a decidedly Georgian character, on landscaped sites where wide grass verges fronted the houses. Many were in areas which were previously empty of such housing, in particular in south Bristol by the Wells road, through Knowle Park, Knowle West and Bedminster Down. Some new houses were built in existing residential areas, like Shirehampton and Seamills. By 1939 there were about 15,000 corporation houses with some 65,000 people living in them.

Early in the Second World War Bristol, over a hundred miles west of London and therefore out of bombing range as it then was, became a refuge and the focus of dispersed employment for many Londoners. Some headquarters staff of the B.B.C. were among these migrants, and the subterranean Clifton Rocks Railway was turned into a studio.

Bristol soon proved to be within the range of German bombers based in northern or north-western France and the city was exposed to bombing attack, particularly in the summer of 1940 and in November of the same year. The raids included a daylight attack on Filton in which many BAC workers were killed. The main damage was in the historic city centre and to some extent in Clifton. 'Area' devastation included Wine Street and St Mary-le-Port Street and surrounding streets in what is now Castle Park. Many churches were burnt out, including St Peter's, St Nicholas's, and St Mary-le-Port; the old parish church in Clifton, All Saints', and St Anselm's were also victims. Among other historic buildings lost or severely damaged were the Dutch House, St Peter's Hospital, the Merchant Venturers' Hall at one end of King Street and the Great Hall in the university. The Temple church was also burnt out, but its famous leaning tower survived. St Mary Reddiffe had some glass blown out, but was structurally unharmed.

At Avonmouth the damage was comparatively light. The docks were important, as in the previous war, for the shipping in of supplies and war material, notably after the entry into the war of the United States. Clifton College, whose staff and boys had moved to Bude, became a headquarters for the United States Army, and was the command post of General Omar Bradley shortly before D-Day, by which time Sir Winston Churchill was Chancellor of the University of Bristol.

Towards the New Millennium

The immediate post-war period in Bristol was one of reconstruction, followed by five decades of immense change to the fabric of the city. A changing townscape was accompanied by equally dramatic changes in community and employment patterns.

As a seafaring city, Bristol has a centuries-old diversity of ethnic backgrounds. The first Jews settled here in the Middle Ages and played an active part in the city's commercial life, most visibly perhaps in Bristol's glass industry, in which Isaac Jacobs was the city's finest craftsman producing the celebrated Bristol blue glass. In the twentieth century, Bristol, along with other British towns, has been a refuge for Jews escaping Nazi persecution in Europe, for Ugandan Asians fleeing Idi Amin and for Vietnamese 'boat people', as well as economic immigrants from all corners of the globe, in particular the West Indies and the Indian sub-continent.

In the closing decades of the century, Bristol's traditional, industry-based economy moved towards greater diversity, with an increased emphasis on 'high-tech' and financial service industries. Although Imperial Tobacco remained based in the city, after the closure of its Hartcliffe plant in the 1990s, cigarettes were no longer manufactured in a city which had been almost synonymous with tobacco. The numbers employed in another traditional Bristol workplace, the docks, also fell, owing to new technology and competition, but after years of losses, there was an unexpectedly happy outcome.

Trade had been declining in the city docks for generations, and the bulk of the city's maritime trade had long since transferred downstream to Avonmouth. In 1975 a new dock, at Portbury, was opened to cater for the growing container traffic. The volume of container business attracted to Bristol did not come up to expectations, and after years of struggle, the City Council bowed to the inevitable. Privatisation in 1991 brought much-needed investment and transformed the docks once again into a vibrant and profitable workplace. By 1998, Bristol was the country's largest car entry port, handling the import of 300,000 cars a year.

In the aeronautical field, Bristol's post-war high spot was the development of Concorde at the BAC Filton

The Bristol Brabazon outside its specially built hangars at Filton; a great feat of engineering, but already overtaken by new technology when it made its maiden flight in 1949.

Concordes undergoing pre-flight servicing at Filton.

complex. At the end of the century, although employment numbers were well down on the peak, Bristol was at the heart of Europe's leading aerospace region. The Ministry of Defence at its Abbey Wood site employed several thou-sands, but the service industries generally provided most new jobs, making Bristol one of the largest financial centres outside London.

In the technological field, Bristol attracted inward

investment by firms like Hewlett Packard and Du Pont Electronics, and also became a magnet for firms wishing to decentralise their operations from London and the crowded South East. Several leading banking and insurance groups settled in the area, attracted by relatively low commercial rents, salaries and other costs, good communications and the quality of life which Bristol could offer their employees.

In the immediate post-war years, Bristol's planners, eager to make a fresh start, took advantage of the wartime destruction in ways much regretted by later generations. Among war-damaged buildings, Park Street – once the West of England's premier shopping area – was rebuilt, but the devastated historic core around Wine Street was abandoned in favour of a new shopping centre in Broadmead. This shift meant the further destruction of buildings which had escaped Hitler's bombs and which would have been protected by the more enlightened conservation policies of later years. In the event, Bristolians lost the physical and emotional heart of their city in favour of one of the drabbest new shopping centres in the country. By the 1990s, buildings of considerably more panache were replacing the jaded mediocrity of the 1960s, not only in Broadmead (now threatened by the development of a massive out-of-town shopping complex outside its northern boundary), but elsewhere in the city's commercial area and, most excitingly, in the former City Docks.

Bristol had lost many fine buildings in the war. Some were rebuilt or restored, like the gutted Great Hall of the University and, in the historic heart, St Nicholas's was restored and fitted out first as a museum of local history and church art and later as a tourist information centre. Other gutted churches were made safe to serve as monuments to the futility of war.

The City Council took the opportunity offered by the Blitz to rehouse thousands who had lived in slum, or near-slum, conditions in the central areas. New housing estates proliferated on the outskirts, continuing the trend which had begun in the 1930s. In the city, waves of new office building in the 1960s and 1970s changed the character and scale of the ancient city and Bristol suffered as badly as any British city from insensitive and badly sited new developments. Among the better new buildings were the Roman Catholic Cathedral in Clifton, built in concrete and granite, the waterfront Lloyds Bank/TSB retail head office of the 1990s and, in Old Market, the purple-brick headquarters of the local newspaper group. But plans for a new harbourside centre for the performing arts which would have given Bristol a building of truly international quality and importance were unexpectedly killed off by the Arts Council, the project's major funder.

Meanwhile, after decades of planning dither, the war-devastated Castle Park area emerged as an attractive new city park, landscaped and adorned with sculpture and artworks by leading contemporary artists and craftspeople.

Although the late 1980s and early 1990s saw a considerable improvement in the quality of the city's new build-

The Roman Catholic Cathedral: one of Bristol's striking twentieth-century buildings.

Aerial view of the city harbour, where work was underway in the late 1990s on the Harbourside project, the largest inner-city regeneration scheme of its day in Europe.

This statue to Raja Ram Mohun Roy near the Central Library was unveiled on 20th November, 1997 to mark the fiftieth anniversary of Indian independence. It was scuplted by Niranjan Pradhan. Roy was an Indian social reformer, noted for campaigning for women's rights, who died on a visit to Bristol in 1833. His exotic Hindu memorial adorns Arno's Vale cemetery in the city.

A striking addition to the city's waterfront: the horn bridge across St Augustine's Reach has been named Pero's Bridge after a black slave of that name.

ings, and a welcome trend to replace some of the worst examples of the post-war period, Bristol's saving grace was the extent and quality of its conservation programme. An enlightened planning authority, encouraged by a strong environmental lobby, oversaw the restoration by sympathetic local architects of much of the largely Georgian fabric of the old city. Notable gains in the city docks included the transformation of a derelict warehouse into the pioneering Arnolfini contemporary arts complex and the conversion of redundant waterside buildings into award-winning residential and leisure-related premises. A significant factor in the success of the transition from moribund docks to a lively 'mix' of uses was the co-operation between public and private sectors and access to central government conservation funds.

Bristol had not been unique in shifting the emphasis in

favour of conservation, but the wholesale restoration of listed buildings in the 1980s had, in one commentator's phrase, transformed Bristol's planning reputation from a national laughing stock into the epitome of sensitive conservation.

By the end of the 1990s, tentative measures to curb the dominance of the car, allied to a programme of pedestrianisation – in historic College Green, Queen Square and elsewhere – had also greatly enhanced the city's central areas. In addition to this, the City Council abandoned its ambivalent attitude to tourism and began vigorously to promote Bristol as a 'great European city'. The new Harbourside development of the arts and sciences, when completed in the early years of the twenty-first century, would complement an architectural urbanity which some years earlier had led John Betjeman to place Bristol ahead of more obvious 'heritage centres' like Bath and York as England's finest city.

Index